The Complete NEWSPAPER RESOURCE BOOK

WESTERN EDUCATIONAL ACTIVITIES LTD.
12006 - 111 Ave., Edmonton, Alberta, T5G 0E6
Ph: (780) 413-7055 Fax: (780) 413-7056
G.S.T. R105012452

J. Weston Walch, Publisher
Portland, Maine

Jane Lamb

ISBN 0-8251-0037-2
Copyright 1985
J. Weston Walch, Publisher
P.O. Box 658 • Portland, Maine 04104-0658

Printed in the United States of America

CONTENTS

PART I

The Newspaper Itself

Chapter 5: Sports, Comics, and Other Special Features 73

Chapter 6: Advertising: More Than Half the Paper 99

PART II

The Newspaper as a Tool for Teaching

LIST OF REPRODUCIBLE PAGES

Chapter 6: Advertising: More Than Half the Paper

Chapter 7: News and History

Chapter 8: The Newspaper Today

Chapter 9: The Newspaper as a Tool for Teaching

TO THE TEACHER

It seems paradoxical that the newspaper itself should lend veracity to the old saying "There's nothing new under the sun." Consider the editorial, reproduced on page xii, from the *Eastern Herald* of June 8, 1795, printed in Portland, Maine. In the two centuries that have elapsed since its publication, thousands of astonishing events have indeed been reported. The world has changed beyond the wildest imaginings that might have occurred to its writer (and not always for the better, despite his belief in the power of the newspaper to "do good to all ranks, denominations, characters and situations in life"). Yet there is little that can be added to his appraisal of the newspaper as the quintessential textbook. Today, as then, the newspaper offers readers of all ages both amusement and information on the widest variety of subjects. It provides daily lessons in living history on the broad scale. At the same time, it is virtually the only chronicle of everyday events in one's own community. It keeps constant watch over the public good and guards with singular zeal our constitutional rights.

Some part of the daily newspaper can "touch the fancy" of the most reluctant reader, especially older students with learning problems, who are embarrassed to use elementary readers for remedial work. With its respected image as an adult medium, the newspaper can motivate them, as well as students without serious problems, to upgrade their reading ability. All kinds of reading and language skills—speed reading, skimming, in-depth reading, critical analysis, vocabulary, spelling, and grammar—can be successfully taught through the newspaper.

Besides its obvious function as a model for journalistic and expository writing, the newspaper is unsurpassed as a source for other writing exercises of all descriptions. It is a treasure chest of topics for panel discussion, debate, dramatics, and other forms of oral English.

Because it is the mirror of society, the newspaper is the ideal text for all branches of social studies. As a day-by-day account of the history of civilization, it can provide the history teacher with a springboard to the past or future. There is no limit to the challenging activities that can be devised from the pages of the newspaper to make geography, economics, sociology, anthropology, or psychology real and important to students.

The world of science claims increasing newspaper space every year. Not only do reports of breakthroughs in medicine, ecology, space, and genetics stimulate interest, but also informative articles frequently suggest practical exercises for the science classroom. Endless possibilities for the math teacher range from finding the perimeter of the front page to writing computer programs.

The arts, which often seem remote from the everyday world, actually receive a fair amount of attention in the newspapers. Students can be asked to read feature stories about artists and reviews of exhibitions and performances that make art and music appreciation a current experience. They can be encouraged to attend those locally available. In addition, the newspaper can be a source for teaching graphic design in the art room or print shop. It is an obvious asset to the photography class.

In our consumer society, the newspaper is the primary source of information on available goods and services, making it useful in teaching consumer education in both the household

ON NEWSPAPERS.

"MUCH has been said and written on the utility of newspapers; but one principal advantage which might be derived from these publications has been neglected; we mean that of reading them in schools, and by the children in families. Try it for one season—Do you wish your child to improve in reading solely, give him a newspaper—it furnishes a variety, some parts of which must infallibly touch his fancy. Do you wish to instruct him in geography, nothing will so indelibly fix the relative situation of different places, as the stories and events published in the papers. In fine, do you wish to have him acquainted with the manners of the country or city, the mode of doing business, public or private; or do you wish him to have a smattering of every kind of science useful and amusing, give him a newspaper—newspapers are plenty and cheap—the cheapest book that can be bought, and the more you buy the better for your children, because every part furnishes some new and valuable information. Instead of being a luxury, it is a matter of economy, and the poorest family, may & ought to be furnished with at least one paper per week. Encourage newspapers and you encourage learning; encourage learning and you secure the liberties of posterity. Learning in the hands of a few, effects a nobility, but generally diffused, is an effectual barrier against every invasion of the rights of man. Newspapers supply the want of schools, the want of company and want of preaching. They have the power to mitigate the pains of the afflicted, alleviate the distresses of the sorrowful, check the wild extravagance of the licentious, bring home the prodigal, and in fine, to do good to all ranks, denominations, characters and situations in life."

From *The Eastern Herald*, June 8, 1795. Printed in Portland, District of Maine, State of Massachusetts. (Reproduced from the original.)

management and home maintenance and construction areas. It provides a wealth of knowledge as well as opportunities to apply practical skills in career education. Students can discover new fields to explore as well as learn how to use the help–wanted ads and to fill out job applications. Even physical education teachers will find uses for the newspaper in articles on health and exercise as well as in articles on the sports page.

In short, the newspaper can help both to develop a whole spectrum of competencies students will be needing for the rest of their lives and to teach them how to use a universal textbook they will be referring to long after those they used in school are forgotten. Teaching through the daily newspaper establishes a two-way street, bringing knowledge of the real world into the classroom and effectually demonstrating that school subjects have practical applications outside the classroom. And the practice keeps teachers themselves more aware of the role that their own subjects play in the wider world, helping to insure the vitality of the curriculum.

The Complete Newspaper Resource Book is designed to make using the newspaper in the classroom easier and more productive for all teachers. It is divided into two sections. Part I, "The Newspaper Itself," contains a comprehensive introduction to the daily newspaper and how it is produced. Subsequent chapters supply more details about all its aspects, including its history and its place in the society of the 1980s, discovered through almost 200 ACTIVITIES. Chapter 7 includes a reproducible booklet on "News and History." Part II, "The Newspaper as a Tool for Teaching," comprises more than 500 ACTIVITIES for individual subject areas, also in separate chapters. A detailed table of contents appears at the beginning of the text; a simplified table of contents, at the beginning of each chapter. One of this book's features is the **Cross-Reference** system, which refers you to ACTIVITIES closely related to the ones you are using, but in other locations of the text. While this is fairly exhaustive, you may, by browsing through the entire book, find still others that will be useful.

You will also find at the back of the book both an APPENDIX, to help you find additional materials, and a BIBLIOGRAPHY of sources and selected reading material for both teacher and students. A GLOSSARY of newspaper terms starts on page 22 at the end of Chapter 1, and a set of GUIDELINES for using this book follows this introduction on page xv. A word of warning: This book *does not* contain a unit on producing a classroom newspaper. Two rather different exercises, however, ACTIVITY 17 on page 39, and the Newspaper in History Project on page 125, give brief experiences in certain aspects of newspaper production.

This book, aimed in the general direction of grades 6 through 12, is, like the newspaper itself, intended to be used selectively. There is a rough logic, but no tightly sequential structure, to the order of chapters in Part I. Feel free to skip around. For some purposes, Chapter 1, "Getting Acquainted with the Newspaper," may be all you ever wanted to know or use on the subject. Or you may want to omit all but Chapter 8, "The Newspaper Today." Some teachers may find it useful to start out with Chapter 5, "Sports, Comics, and Other Special Features," as a non-threatening introduction. Do have a look at the others, however.

ACTIVITIES in each chapter, arranged for the most part in order of increasing sophistication, are also intended to be selected and adapted. They are to be regarded not as a course outline, but as idea starters. You will very likely think of more, even better, ones yourself, and for this purpose, SPACE FOR YOUR IDEAS is provided at the end of each chapter.

In Part I, an EVALUATION section at the end of each chapter includes QUIZZES and other reproducible material. (Additional pages that can be reproduced appear in certain chapters. All are marked **[R]**.) There are also some sample tests for adaptation to specific time, place, and individual needs. No attempt has been made to provide QUIZZES for Part II, since there is no way of telling which ACTIVITIES you will select or how you will use them.

QUIZZES and ACTIVITIES throughout are designed to provoke critical thinking. Many assignments require the use of library and other research methods similar to those used by professional journalists. Students will be surprised to discover the vast amount of research that goes into producing a newspaper. One feature writer has remarked that she writes several "term papers" a week in the course of her work.

Newspapers for use in the classroom (as well as help of other kinds) can usually be obtained at a reduced rate from one of the daily newspapers serving your area. More than 600 newspapers in the United States and Canada cooperate in the Newspaper in Education (NIE) program of the American Newspaper Publishers Association Foundation and the Canadian Daily Newspaper Publishers Association. NIE has extensive material available to help teachers and students use the newspaper for learning. (See APPENDIX for addresses.) National Newspaper in Education Week comes in early March each year. State departments of education have various Newspaper in Education programs. As of 1984, Maine and Florida are the only states with full-time consultants providing such services as training workshops, curriculum materials, classroom visits, and individual consultations in program development. They also offer programs for parent/school organizations which help parents focus on the newspaper as a way of helping children at home. (See APPENDIX.) Local services, such as tours of newspaper plants, speakers' bureaus, and printed materials are often provided by daily newspapers.

The purpose of this book is to bring together material from as many sources as possible—including the author's long experience as a classroom teacher and freelance journalist—not as a textbook, but as a tool and sourcebook for teachers using the newspaper in the classroom. The newspaper itself is a textbook for all seasons or, as it has often been called, a "living textbook."

As comprehensive as this book tries to be, however, there is no way to anticipate the many unique possibilities and one-of-a-kind curiosities the news of the day may bring to your classroom. Perhaps the best teaching tool of all is an alert eye for such gems that, with your creative application, will make today's lesson come alive.

—Jane Lamb

GENERAL GUIDELINES
For Teachers Using the Newspaper in the Classroom

Use this book selectively. It is not a course, but a collection of ideas

See Contents list at the beginning of text for subjects of activities.

Follow up *Cross References* given throughout to related ACTIVITIES in other parts of the book.

Create and record your own ACTIVITIES in the SPACE FOR YOUR IDEAS provided at the end of each chapter.

Keep an alert eye for news items that will make today's lesson as up-to-the-minute, alive, and exciting as possible.

Give regular assignments related to the latest news in your subject area.

Keep a clipping file on your subject (and others of interest). Check the papers daily, and add to it regularly.

See APPENDIX for sources of useful information and aids. Educational films and filmstrips are listed by the chapter to which they relate.

Contact your local newspaper and all services connected with the Newspaper in Education (NIE) program of the American Newspaper Publishers Association Foundation for additional help.

Note that National Newspaper in Education week comes in early March.

ACKNOWLEDGMENTS

The author wishes to express appreciation to the many individuals and organizations who have so kindly given advice or permission to use their materials.

First, a very special thank you to James L. Abbott, former consultant to the Maine State Newspaper in Education Program, now NIE coordinator for the Guy Gannett Newspapers, Portland, Maine, for his support, encouragement, and generous offer of materials.

Next, to the American Newspaper Publishers Association Foundation Newspaper in Education program for permission to use many of their materials, particularly to adapt from their publication *The Newspaper as an Effective Teaching Tool* ACTIVITIES 2, 25, 26, and 114 in Chapter 9 and ACTIVITIES 40, 51, 80, and 114 in Chapter 11. Also to the Canadian Daily Newspaper Publishers Association for permission to use ACTIVITY 80 in Chapter 9.

And to all of the following:

Richard G. Gray, dean, and Trevor R. Brown, associate dean, Indiana University School of Journalism, for their invaluable teaching of the history and practice of newspaper work; Alfred J. Wilson, principal of the Marshall School, Granite City, Illinois, for his enthusiastic response and encouragement; Jack Gillespie of Glassboro Teachers College, Glassboro, New Jersey, for permission to adapt sports section activities and APPENDIX materials from *Getting Started. . .in Journalism*, by Jack Gillespie and Herschel O. Engebretson, Glassboro, N.J., Educational Impact, 1973; Michael Harmon, assistant managing editor of the *Portland* (Maine) *Press Herald*, for permission to use his column "Newspaper's Challenge Is to Be Fast—and Fair" in Chapter 8; the Portland (Maine) Public Library for permission to use the excerpt from the *Eastern Herald* of June 8, 1795, in "To the Teacher"; the *New England Reading Association Journal* for permission to use quotes from Dr. Carl Sailer's "The Place of Newspaper Reading in Reading Instruction," Summer 1966 issue, in Chapter 1; John Wiley and Sons Inc., for permission to reprint "A Classic Account of Bull Run" from *Voices of the Past* by Calder M. Pickett; the *Maine Times*, the *Portland Press Herald*, and the Brunswick, Maine, *Times Record* for permission to use headlines and lead paragraphs in Chapter 2; Yankee Pedaler Bicycles, Inc., for permission to use their advertisement, "Yikes! Great Bikes," in Chapter 6; and Nancy L. Nelson for permission to reprint her article, "Take Metaphors Out of Journalism's Sails," originally printed in the *Los Angeles Times*, in Chapter 9.

PART I
The Newspaper Itself

Getting Acquainted
with the Newspaper

CONTENTS

A NEWSPAPER LEARNING STATION

A newspaper learning station in your classroom can add excitement and motivation to many activities and can be easily constructed. An example of one such station, created by the Newspaper in Education staff at the *Minneapolis Star & Tribune*, is pictured above. Some suggestions for using a newspaper learning station are listed below:

1. Create activity cards from teaching suggestions in this book or from your own ideas. Select activities carefully to reinforce concepts and skills you are teaching.

2. Establish with the help of students some guidelines for using the station:

   A. Times the station may be used.

   B. Number of students who may be at the station at one time.

   C. Acceptable behavior rules and penalties for violation.

   D. How or if newspaper activities will be graded.

Getting Acquainted with the Newspaper

The importance of establishing a lifelong habit of effectual newspaper reading is clear enough to the teacher, but students may have to be convinced. Among the following approaches, gleaned from the experience of many successful teachers, you should find one that will turn on a particular class, or perhaps spark a creative adaptation of your own. Dr. Carl Sailer[1] recommends that teachers consider the following points in developing a newspaper unit.

- Center the work around the commonly read daily newspaper.

- Use a wide range of materials and newspapers.[2]

- Plan topics cooperatively, the teacher helping the students to choose the areas to be studied and the questions to be raised.

- Guide study into class, group, and individual projects.

- Use panels of students.

- Include a great deal of discussion, informal and semi-formal.

I. PRE-UNIT TEASER

ACTIVITY

1. Place on your classroom bulletin board three displays:

   - Pictures of personalities in the news, without captions, under the heading "Who am I?"

   - News stories under the heading "Where in the world or in space did this happen?"

   - News stories under the heading "Why on earth or in space did this happen?"

   - Leave the display up for about a week, making it clear that students are expected to find the answers. Offer no information except to answer questions about where to look. At the end of the week give a test on the displays.

---

[1]In "The Place of Newspaper Reading in Reading Instruction," *Journal of the New England Reading Association*, Summer 1966.

[2]For information on how to obtain newspapers for classroom use, see APPENDIX.

One of the most painless ways to launch a newspaper unit is simply to reinforce "doing what comes naturally." Pass out newspapers to the class and tell them to read whatever they want to, allowing them fifteen or twenty minutes. Those who finish in less than five may find themselves venturing into unknown territory while they wait for their classmates to finish. The discussion that follows can go almost anywhere. For further details needed to answer questions that might come up, consult the TABLE OF CONTENTS or the APPENDIX.

II. GETTING ACQUAINTED

ACTIVITIES

2. Take an informal survey* of what students turn to first in this preliminary reading. Make it quite clear that there is nothing sinful about heading straight for the sports section or the comics. Students will be giving closer attention to these important pages, along with other newspaper departments, in the near future. Take time to hear arguments for their priorities and to ask why the sections of the newspaper that no one in the class read are printed at all.

3. Ask how many are currently newspaper readers, what parts they read, and how much time they spend on the paper every day. If TV news is brought up as a substitute, this will be a good time to make preliminary comparison between TV and printed news coverage, or you may want to defer this discussion to a more in-depth analysis when you take up Chapter 8, "The Newspaper Today" (which see for detailed comparison).

4. Have students keep a newspaper-reading journal for a week, recording how much time they spend and listing the articles they have read. At the end of the week, compare notes. Which topics interested the most students, no matter which newspaper they might have found them in? Why? At the end of the unit, you might go back to these journals to discover whether increased familiarity has changed any habits.

III. VALUES OF NEWSPAPER READING

ACTIVITY

5. Hold a brainstorming session on the value of newspaper reading. Challenge the class to make the longest possible list of reasons for reading the newspaper. Have them decide which are the most important and why. Here you may want to bring in some of the rationale suggested in the INTRODUCTION. What should emerge in some form, however, are the basic contributions the newspaper makes to everyday life:

---

*If you wish to use a written survey, a sample is included in the EVALUATION section at the end of the chapter.

- Information on a tremendous variety of subjects, current and perennial; local, national and international

- Interpretation of events and issues, by everyone from the students' own neighbors (in letters to the editor and interviews) to widely acknowledged experts.

- Services that help them solve problems of business, home, recreation, daily living; services that help the business community carry out its regular transactions. Many of these services are performed by the advertisements.

- Entertainment, stimulation, diversion, and enjoyment.

Or, to put it another way, becoming a better newspaper reader can help students to be well informed, to form intelligent opinions, and to enjoy life.

IV. SOME MORE STARTERS

ACTIVITIES

6. Have students create posters demonstrating these contributions, all four or individually. For example, a poster might illustrate how the following meet people's needs:

   - Help Wanted—typist seeking work
   - Obituaries—elderly person concerned about friends
   - Consumer Ads—housewife doing comparative food shopping
   - Real Estate—family with six children looking for housing

7. Another way to get started is to begin with the biggest news story of the moment, anywhere from hometown to overseas: a major sports event, a political crisis, a scientific breakthrough, a human interest drama. Compare its coverage in several different newspapers, by their own staff or by the wire services. This can lead in many directions: to news sources, layout of the front page, bias (all given more detailed treatment below).

8. One educator[1] suggests beginning a newspaper unit with the advertisements, their meaning and interpretation.[2] Students are eager to learn how to recognize a bargain and get their money's worth. Teachers can use this approach as a springboard not only to the newspaper unit, but also to consumer education (Chapter 14), economics (Chapter 11, V), math (Chapter 13), language and semantics (Chapter 9, II A) or the psychology used by ad writers (Chapter 11, V B). For everyone, the game of marketplace oneupmanship is fun.

---

[1]Carl Sailer, *op. cit.*
[2]See Chapter 6, "Advertising: More Than Half the Paper."

V. THE FRONT PAGE

Of course, you can always begin in the most obvious place, the front page.

ACTIVITIES

9. Using the daily paper, have students first count the number of stories on the front page and then make some elementary observations.

Are all the stories on different topics, or are some on the same or closely related topics? Why?

Are all written in the same style? Discuss the simple differences between **spot** news (concerning events occurring within the last 24 hours), or **hard** news (stories containing straight factual material) and **feature** stories (background, human interest, or other information not so dependent on the time element, often more imaginatively written). These will be treated in detail in Chapters 2 and 3.

Where did the stories come from? Have students find examples of:

- Staff-written stories originating locally or sent from out of town by an assigned staff member.

- Wire service stories from the Associated Press (AP), a cooperative, non-profit organization of American newspapers; or from United Press International (UPI), a commercial newsgathering organization.

- Syndicated news services such as those of the *New York Times*, the *Chicago Tribune*, the *Christian Science Monitor,* or foreign news services such as the British Reuters.

- Local correspondents or "stringers," who keep the paper posted on events in their territories for a regular stipend, but are not staff members; freelance writers, usually of features, who are paid by the individual story.

- News releases, prepared stories issued by public relations departments of civic and cultural organizations and government agencies.

Why are the stories arranged as they are? Usually it's according to the editor's estimate of their importance. Traditional positions are:

- Lead story (most important): upper right.

- Second lead: upper left.

- Other important stories above the fold line (so they will be seen as the paper lies in the pile on the newsstand).

10. Have students list every other detail they find on the front page.* These should include:

Flag (nameplate or banner): the newspaper's name.

---

*A sample front page to be used either for illustration or as a quiz (by substituting blanks for terms in list) can be found on page 17.

Ears: small boxes at either side of the flag which may contain the price, the weather, or words of wisdom, or even be absent altogether.

Skyline: a headline above the flag at the top of the page, often calling attention to news on inside pages.

Border: the line just below the flag which usually contains the day's date, the city, the volume and number of the issue, copyright, number of pages, price or a slogan (such as "All the News That's Fit to Print").

Headline (head): the main facts of the story below it.

- Screamer (streamer, banner): head that runs the full width of the page

Kicker: word or short phrase above the headline, in a different type size, giving added information or emphasis.

- Hanger: smaller-type-size headline below main head, giving added details.

Byline: identifies the writer of the story. Some papers use a great many; others reserve them for stories that represent the writer's interpretation or special knowledge of the subject.

Dateline: gives the place the story originated and the reporting news agency, but seldom the date. The term originated in earlier times before instant satellite communication. The date appeared after the place name because a story might be printed anywhere from a day to several weeks (in the days of sail, for example) after it was written.

Box(es): bordered item, sometimes in a different typeface, to call attention to important information.

Pictures (cuts, pics or pix): note whether they were taken by a staff photographer or sent by wire service (found in **credit line**).

Refer (pronounced reefer): reference to news on inside pages.

Index: lists contents of inner pages.

Filler: several lines of trivial information used to fill empty space.

Individual newspapers have their own front-page specialties.

VI. HOW TO READ A NEWSPAPER*

To make the most effective use of the newspaper, students need to learn to locate materials quickly by using the index, by skimming, by scanning; they must learn to read rapidly, at a normal rate, and intensively. TIPS FOR GETTING THE MOST FROM YOUR NEWSPAPER, a reproducible guide on page 8, will help students develop these various reading skills. A variety of games can be invented to sharpen these skills. A few follow, but many have to be tailored to individual news items.

*Cross Reference: Chapter 9, "English": I. Reading, A. Comprehension

Name _____ Date _____

TIPS FOR GETTING THE MOST FROM YOUR NEWSPAPER

There are several ways to read a newspaper, but whatever method you choose, be sure it is systematic. By following the same pattern every day, you will avoid missing important news. Form the habit of reading the paper at the same time every day. You may only have time to skim it before breakfast, read a few stories at lunch, and spend a bit longer in the evening in serious reading. Here are some shortcuts to help you get the most from the paper in your crowded day.

1.   Skim the entire paper, reading every headline and picture caption. You won't know all the news, but you'll have an idea about it. In the few minutes it takes you to skim, make mental notes of the articles you want to return to.

2.   Read your major interests first. Once these are satisfied, motivation for further reading changes. Now you can study the news more carefully.

3.   Read the front-page stories. This is where the editors have placed the most important news. You can get the major facts from the lead, where the Five Ws summarize the story. On a busy day, you may not have time for more.

4.   Read the inside pages. Your opinion of what the major news stories are may not be the same as the editor's. Today's inside-page stories may be tomorrow's front-page stories. Nobody could read all of the newspaper. There's enough reading matter in a single day's issue to fill a medium-size book. Now is the time to think of the mental notes you made while skimming and to return to the stories you wanted to read later.

5.   Read the editorials, columnists, and letters to the editor last, when you have time to give serious thought to the opinions expressed. The editorial page is intended to stimulate the reader. Letters to the editor will also give you an idea how other readers feel on certain issues. Most controversial editorials arouse quick response from people who do not agree with the paper's position.

(Adapted from *Your Daily Newspaper*, James L. Abbott, ed., Newspaper in Education, Maine Department of Educational and Cultural Services)

ACTIVITIES

11. Have students use the index to locate "Dear Abby," sports, editorials, classifieds, horoscope, comics, financial pages. This could be made a speed contest if desired.

12. Scavenger hunts offer endless opportunities for gathering information, developing vocabulary, or just getting acquainted with the paper.[1]

13. Prepare several questions relating to a current issue of the paper (see sample worksheets at the end of this chapter). Vary questions, so that some answers can be found by quickly skimming, some require more in-depth reading, and some demand that students make inferences from the material. Students could answer these questions either orally or as a written assignment. Afterwards, discuss how each answer was found.[2]

14. After a half-hour reading session, have students make up a Crazy Quiz of picky questions, then have the class take a composite test on them.

15. Have students survey a single day's issue of the newspaper and list articles of interest to different people: those younger than themselves, their own age group, young adults, business people, homemakers, retired people. What conclusions can they draw? Some possibilities:

    - The newspaper is for everybody.

    - There's a lot in the paper they'll never see on TV.

    - They'll probably be reading the paper for the rest of their lives. It would be a good idea to know how to get the most out of it.

VII. WHAT MAKES A GOOD NEWSPAPER?

What makes a good newspaper? A bad one? The question of whether newspapers are worth bothering with at all may have come up in the discussion of the values of newspaper reading. Students may express the opinion (or that of their parents) that newspapers are biased, that they report only bad news, that there is no truth to be found in them.

Bias, real or imagined, is one of the chronic complaints against any source of information, most particularly the news media, whose influence is so pervasive. There was a time when "objectivity" was widely regarded as the highest ideal of journalism. Today serious journalists generally concede the impossibility of discovering and reporting "objective truth." Indeed, the very nature of truth is the ultimate philosophical question. "Truth" varies with time, place and point of view.[3] Eric Severeid, one of America's most respected journalists,

---

[1] For sample scavenger hunts, see EVALUATION section, pp. 18, 19.

[2] For sample quizzes, see EVALUATION section at end of chapter, pp. 20, 21.

[3] J. Bronowski explores this hypothesis interestingly in Chapter 11, "Knowledge or Certainty," of his widely-read book, *The Ascent of Man* (Little, Brown and Co., Boston, 1973). The TV series by the same name, repeated frequently on public television, presents this idea with great clarity.

has said that the greatest fault in news reporting is not bias, but haste. "The theory of the free press is that the full truth is not revealed in one account, but emerges through free reporting and discussion. The central point is not fairness nor accuracy, but **freedom**, which makes the others possible."[1] (Freedom of the press will be given fuller treatment in Chapters 7, 8, and 11.)

Commercial newspapers (most newspapers) are businesses, part of what is known as the "newspaper industry," a national institution of gigantic proportions. Newspaper publishers (owners) are first and foremost business people. Like all responsible members of the business community, they intend to serve the public fairly and honestly, but like all human beings, they see the world according to their own experience and best interests. Publishers are not necessarily journalists themselves, though many smaller newspapers are owner/editor operations, and many publishers are or have been professional journalists. Most, if not all, are interested in the power and influence of their newspaper and its role in shaping public opinion. The professional journalists hired by publishers as editors and reporters may be more directly engaged in seeking the truth than their employers, but they also work within the editorial policy of the publication. This cannot help but result in different publications' representing different points of view, a far more interesting and healthy situation than if all were alike, either for lack of lively investigative curiosity or because of government control. Even the same wire service story may be given different emphasis in different newspapers. (See ACTIVITIES 17 and 18 on page 11.)

In the days, now almost vanished, when every fair-sized city boasted at least two rival newspapers representing different commercial, political, or cultural interests, conflict could be dramatic: lively battles were often waged, the likes of which are unknown among the all-but-identical TV network news programs. But even today, the well-informed citizen can gain the clearest understanding of important events and issues by getting the news from more than one paper, as well as by noting radio and television coverage. As Eric Severeid suggests, the truth, or at least a more balanced perspective, eventually emerges.

VIII. WHAT KINDS OF NEWSPAPERS ARE OUT THERE?

While differences in newspapers will doubtless come up in discussion, students will gain a better appreciation of them through some hands-on discovery. Make available a wide range of newspapers: local, state, national; dailies, weeklies, monthlies. Have students bring from home others that may be available there, including trade, house, and special-interest publications.

ACTIVITY

16. Work with students to create a display with this collection representing as many of the following categories as possible.[2]

    Frequency of publication:

    – Dailies

    – Weeklies and bi-weeklies

    – Monthlies

---

[1]From an address given at Indiana University in 1978.

[2]A quiz on this material can be found in the EVALUATION section at the end of the chapter.

– Quarterlies and annuals, which are usually regarded as magazines, or, if of a professional nature, oddly enough, "journals." Remind students of the derivation of "journal" and hence, "journalism." (See any good dictionary.)

Type of news coverage:

– General: most dailies, weeklies, some monthlies, large or small.

– Special interest: for example, sports, high school papers, farming.

– Trade journals: for specific businesses and professions.

– House organs: produced by a company for its employees or customers.

Type of approach:

– General: full-size papers which treat a wide range of subjects in serious detail, using the most reliable news sources and appealing to better educated readers.

– Tabloid: half the size of standard newspapers, with briefer articles, more photos, easier to read for people in a hurry or with less interest in depth.

– Sensational or "yellow"* journals: those emphasizing the melodramatic side of the news, often taking extreme political stands.

– Underground: anti-establishment newspapers, representing minority views running counter to the cultural mainstream.

IX. COMPARING DIFFERENT NEWSPAPERS

ACTIVITIES

17. Post front pages of several different newspapers of the same date. Ask students to check how many of the same stories are used. Which papers either do not use a story used by several others or put it on another page? Why? One of the commonest forms of bias is "slanting by selection of facts," which may be a matter of honest, not necessarily sinister, priorities. Students should notice, however, that unpopular or controversial subjects have a way of getting lost on page 76, among the used car ads.

18. Find the same story in several papers and observe differences in treatment. Are all from wire services or do some papers send a staff reporter? Why? (Possibilities include size of staff, estimate of importance.) Do they emphasize the same details? Have students compare placement on page and headlines, and ask them to draw as many inferences as possible from this information. Here again, both bias by selection and placement of facts should be considered.

---

*"Yellow journalism" got its name from the "Yellow Kid," a popular cartoon character in William Randolph Hearst's sensational *New York Journal* in the 1890s.

19. Using several papers, have students compare:

    - Ratio of news to advertising. (The ratio varies from 50–50 for small papers to as much as 70 percent advertising to 30 percent news for large papers of 75 to 100 pages. It is considered financially unhealthy to fall below 50 percent advertising.)

    - Ratio of hard news to feature material. (Depends on the paper's purpose and/or audience.)

    - Ratio of wire service and syndicated materials to staff-written materials. (A large amount of wire service and syndicated material may mean a low budget. These services are usually cheaper than staff salaries and their accompanying fringe benefits.)[1]

20. Have students compare editorials on the same subject in two or more papers.

21. Have students compare staff-written material in two different papers with an eye to style and quality of writing. What differences do they find? Which writers do they prefer? Why?

22. Have students find the same stories in several papers and examine the headlines with attention to choice of details highlighted and the use of words with negative, positive, or fairly neutral connotation. If you question "fairly" neutral, just challenge anyone to come up with a noun or verb that has absolutely **no** connotative color whatever.[2]

23. On the editorial page, find an editorial on the same subject as a news story on the front page. Have students decide whether the reporter or the headline writer in any way reflects the view of the editorial writer. Most newspapers try to keep these departments sharply separated. Do they always succeed?

24. Compare the visual effects of various publications:[3]

    - Loud, splashy   - Offbeat, innovative
    - Quiet, conservative   - Tasteless or sloppy
    - Graphically distinctive - Dull

    Have students decide whether these reflect the editorial content.

25. Compare stories on the same subject in daily and weekly papers. You may wish to include weekly or monthly news and public affairs magazines as well. Ask students to find differences in treatment and explain why these occur. Ask if they discern any evidence to support Severeid's observation about haste.

---

[1] **Cross Reference:** Chapter 13, "Math"

[2] **Cross Reference:** Chapter 9, "English": II. Language, A. Semantics

[3] **Cross Reference:** Chapter 2, "What Is News?": VI. Layout; Chapter 10, "The Arts": II. Visual Arts, A. Graphics

X. CRITERIA FOR A GOOD NEWSPAPER

ACTIVITY

26. After completing several of the preceding activities, ask students to compile a list of criteria for a good newspaper. Some widely accepted standards are:

    - Adequate and concise coverage of important news.

    - Sense of news value. (This will be treated in detail in Chapter 2.)

    - Amount of news compared to amount of advertising.

    - Number of staff correspondents nationally and abroad compared to dependence on wire services.

    - Accuracy and appropriateness of headlines.

    - Unbiased reporting and editing.

    - Variety and balance of contents.

    - Responsibility of editorials.

    - Broad spectrum of columnists, both staff and syndicated.

By the time they have finished the entire unit, students will have a much better appreciation of the meaning of these criteria. The question of what ought and ought not to be printed is dealt with in detail in the discussion of the First Amendment in THE FREE PRESS in Chapter 11, "Social Studies," and briefly elsewhere.

XI. PRODUCING THE NEWSPAPER

How does the newspaper happen? The best way to find out is to arrange a visit to a nearby daily newspaper. Many papers conduct tours of their plants for students on a regular basis and will be extremely cooperative. In addition, or alternatively, you might invite a member of the newspaper staff to talk to the class. In rural areas, the local correspondent to the nearest weekly or daily newspaper might be a willing and helpful guest. Audiovisual materials are also available.[1] Make sure they are up to date. Newspaper production has been going through some profound technological changes in recent years, and some AV materials are hopelessly antiquated, as are some high school textbooks on the subject. Whichever of the above activities you are able to arrange, a basic understanding of the process will prepare students to ask more pertinent questions.

ACTIVITY

27. Students or teacher might set up a bulletin board display illustrating the steps from news event to front page.[2] A brief outline follows.

---

[1] See APPENDIX for sources.

[2] A flow chart would be an interesting alternative to an illustrated display.

– **Something happens** that's newsworthy. If it's unexpected, a fire or an accident, for example, witnesses may phone the paper, but most newsrooms monitor police calls and send a reporter out at once. If the event is expected—a town meeting, the Academy Awards—reporters have already been assigned to "cover" the story. Sources of constant news, such as city hall, the state house, and the United Nations are regular "beats" of specific reporters.

– **The reporter writes** or "files" a story either by phone from the scene of the event or at a desk in the paper's newsroom. If the reporter works instead for one of the wire services, the same is done in the wire service office, and the story is sent out to all subscribing newspapers.

– In the newsroom, **the city or copy editor assigns the story** to a copy reader, who checks it for length, style, and accuracy and then writes a headline. The copy editor also selects stories of local interest from the wire service and assigns them to copy readers. Today most reporters type their stories directly into a computer which displays their work on a video screen above their keyboard. They can correct and rewrite as they go along. The apparatus is a type of word processor, usually referred to as the **VDT (Video Display Terminal)**. When the story is finished, it is sent to the editor's terminal, where it is checked and sent directly to the composing room.

– **In the composing room** the story, with its headline, is automatically printed on a strip of paper by a photographic process. Newspaper pages are made up by pasting the stories, along with ads produced by a similar process, on page-size sheets. This step is called **pasteup**. Editors responsible for different pages plan the design or **layout** for these pasteups and frequently go to the composing room to approve them for printing. (The most up-to-date technology can even produce whole pages electronically, without preliminary pasteup.)*

– **A huge camera is used to photograph each page** and the resulting negative is used to transfer the page to a thin aluminum **press plate** coated with light-sensitive material. In the photographic process, the exposed coating serves as a resist for protecting the image areas (the areas to be printed) while the non-image areas are etched in an acid bath.*

– Plates for every page of the paper go to the **press room**, where they are attached to the cylinders of a giant press, often two stories high. It is called a web press because the paper runs in a single strip from a huge roll through a series of cylinders that print the pages.

– **As the pages come off the press they are automatically cut, folded, and bundled,** ready for the delivery truck to take them to the newsstands and the post office, or for the individual carriers who distribute them to local businesses and homes to pick them up.

---

*See APPENDIX for sources of more technical details.

XII. HOW NEWSPAPERS USED TO BE PRINTED

This slick process, made possible by rapid advances in electronic technology, is considerably different from the standard newspaper production methods of only a few years ago, which are still practiced in various stages of modernization by many newspapers, large and small. Almost entirely gone (in newspaper printing at least) are the rows of clicking **linotype** machines in the composing room, where typesetters sat at keyboards setting stories line by line and casting them in type metal. Each line of type was called a **slug**. The tray in which the entire story was placed was called a **galley**. A **proof** was made by placing a piece of paper over the inked type and running a roller across it by hand. This **galley proof** was sent back to the newsroom where a **proofreader** checked it for errors. Reporters and copywriters in a modern newsroom, typing stories at the VDT, do their own typesetting, editing, and proofreading, eliminating several steps in the time-honored process and at the same time becoming as much technicians as journalists. Most newspaper people over the age of 30 have seen all these changes take place. Students might ask some of them how they feel about these changes.

Headlines, at one time set by hand, one letter at a time, were later cast in slugs by a machine similar to a linotype equipped with several larger sizes of type. Only after galley proofs were corrected and OK'd were stories, along with their headlines and advertising, locked into the **chase** (a heavy steel frame). A page proof was then made and checked again for errors.*

ACTIVITIES

28. Students with a particular interest in graphics might want to investigate and report in further detail on the various methods used to transfer these type metal pages to curved plates to be installed on the printing press. The teacher should also remind students that many variations of the "old-fashioned" printing methods described above are still used to produce magazines, books, and other printed matter of all kinds.

29. As a final assignment for this chapter, you might ask students to write a news article about their trip to the newspaper plant, the visit of the newspaper professional, or the film they have seen. These articles should reveal how much they already understand about newswriting style, indicating at what level you need to begin activities in Chapter 2.

XIII. CHAPTER EVALUATION

Many of the activities in this chapter can be used as written assignments, projects, or tests for purposes of evaluation. In addition, quizzes and other activities referred to in the text can be found on the following pages.

---

*A quiz on newspaper production terms can be found in the EVALUATION section on page 21.

Name _____ Date _____

NEWSPAPER SURVEY

1. **How often do you read a newspaper?**

    _____ **Every day**   _____ **Occasionally**   _____ **Rarely**

2. **How much time (hours per day) do you spend reading a newspaper?** _____

    Watching television? _____   **Listening to the radio?** _____

3. **Where do you get the day's news?**

    _____ **Newspaper**   _____ **Radio**

    _____ **Television**   _____ **Don't get it at all**

4. **What part of the newspaper did you turn to first today? Indicate your preference by using (1) for the part you read first, (2) for the part you read second, (3) for the part you read third.**

    _____ **Ann Landers/Dear Abby**   _____ **Local news**

    _____ **Comics**   _____ **Obituaries**

    _____ **Crossword puzzle**   _____ **Sports**

    _____ **Editorials**   _____ **Syndicated columnists**

    _____ **Feature section**   _____ **TV and radio**

    _____ **Editorial cartoons**   _____ **Want ads**

    _____ **Financial**   _____ **Weather forecast**

    _____ **Front page**   _____ **Weddings and engagements**

    _____ **Letters to the editor**   _____ **Other (name)** _____

5. **What do you enjoy most about newspapers?**

6. **What do you enjoy least about newspapers?**

SAMPLE FRONT PAGE

1 Skyline

2 Flag (banner, nameplate)

3 Ears

4 Border

5 Screamer (banner, streamer)

6 Headline

7 Dateline

8 Cut (photo, pic, pix)

9 Cutline (caption)

10 Byline

11 Kicker

12 Refer (pronounced "reefer")

13 Hanger

14 Box

15 Index

Name _____ Date _____

SCAVENGER HUNT
(for teams of two to four)

How many of these things can you find in the newspaper? When you find one of the items, you must do two things: 1 – put the page number on this list and 2 – circle the item in the newspaper. Good luck!

_____	Today's date
_____	Two prices in a single advertisement that total $12.98
_____	A number larger than one million
_____	Television schedules
_____	The weather report
_____	An abbreviation
_____	An opinion
_____	A food you like to eat
_____	A used car for sale
_____	A verb in a headline
_____	A puzzle
_____	A question mark
_____	A house for sale
_____	The name of a country
_____	An acronym
_____	The president's name
_____	The name of the governor of your state
_____	A movie you would like to see
_____	The name of a singer
_____	The name of your town
_____	A news story from your state capital
_____	Something you can buy for 99¢
_____	A picture of a person
_____	Your favorite cartoon
_____	The name of a sports team

A VERY ACTIVE SCAVENGER HUNT
(for teams of three to five)

This is a race. It will get you around in the newspaper, but the prime objective is group organization and the procedures for getting the job done. Teamwork is the key. Hurry, hurry!

MATERIALS NEEDED: *scissors, paste, newspapers, 1 large piece of paper per group*

FIND, CUT and PASTE one sample for each item listed below.

1. A number greater than a million

2. The high temperature in a major city

3. The price of meat per pound

4. A face with glasses

5. An international dateline

6. An animal either pictured or mentioned. Next to this item, list the names of the people in the group who have ever touched one of these animals.

7. Illustrate a sports headline. (Stick figures allowed. Be quick. This isn't art!)

8. The price of a used Mustang

9. A game

10. A letter from someone

11. A city within 100 miles of your present location

12. A number smaller than one (1)

13. A column (a regular feature by a particular writer)

14. A vehicle other than a car

15. Something to play with

16. A movie that starts between 7 and 9 p.m.

17. A compound word

18. An angry word

19. A TV channel that broadcasts a 6 p.m. news program

20. A job you'd like to apply for

AS SOON AS YOU'VE FINISHED, STAND UP AND YELL, "WE'RE DONE, WE'RE DONE!"

Name _____ Date _____

———— QUIZ ON TYPES OF NEWSPAPERS ————
for ACTIVITY 16, pages 10–11

Use the bulletin board display of publications collected from a wide range of sources as the point of reference.

1. _____ and _____ are examples of

   general interest dailies.

2. A tabloid is characterized by _____ size and is often

   preferred by readers because _____

   and _____ .

3. _____ is an example of a house organ. It is pub-

   lished for _____ .

4. Weekly news magazines such as _____ and

   _____ provide a different view of the news

   because _____ .

   How do monthly news magazines compare? _____

   _____ .

5. _____ is an example of a trade journal. Trade

   journals are read by _____ .

6. _____ is an example of a sensational publication. Explain

   what is meant by "yellow journalism." _____

   _____ .

7. _____ is an example of an "underground" publication.

   Why is it so labeled? _____

   _____ .

Name _____   _____ Date _____

___ QUIZ ON NEWSPAPER PRODUCTION TERMS ___

*In the blank before each item in Column A write the letter of the description in
Column B that best fits it.*

A	**B**
___ 1. Cover	a. Frame that holds a page of metal type in place for printing
___ 2. Beat	b. Design of newspaper pages
___ 3. File	c. Metal tray to hold type
___ 4. Wire service	d. Attaching stories and ads to page for printing
___ 5. Slotman, city editor	e. To get information on an event for a news story
___ 6. Copy reader	f. Controls many aspects of modern newspaper production
___ 7. VDT	g. Machine that casts metal type in lines
___ 8. Composing room	h. Single line of cast metal type
___ 9. Pasteup	i. Organization that collects news and sends it to local papers
___ 10. Layout	j. Territory that a single reporter covers regularly
___ 11. Press plate	k. Print of a page to be checked before going to press
___ 12. Web press	l. Screen on word processor where story appears as it is typed
___ 13. Galley	m. Person who reads and edits stories, writes headlines
___ 14. Linotype	n. To send or give a news story to your paper
___ 15. Proofreader	o. Print of a story to be checked before going to press
___ 16. Slug	p. Press that prints many pages on a single strip of paper
___ 17. Chase	q. Where stories and ads get put together on pages
___ 18. Computer	r. Person who checks typeset material for errors
___ 19. Galley proof	s. Person who assigns and approves news stories
___ 20. Page proof	t. Plate from which newspaper page is printed

© 1985 J. Weston Walch, Publisher

ANSWERS TO QUIZ ON
—————— NEWSPAPER PRODUCTION TERMS ———————

1. e		11. t	
2. j		12. p	
3. n		13. c	
4. i		14. g	
5. s		15. r	
6. m		16. h	
7. l		17. a	
8. q		18. f	
9. d		19. o	
10. b		20. k	

XIV. GLOSSARY OF NEWSPAPER TERMINOLOGY

AD — advertisement

ADD — more material to be added to story

ADVANCE — story about coming events

ANGLE — approach to a news story

AP — abbreviation for Associated Press

ASSIGNMENT — story a reporter has to cover

BALLOON — In comics, circle enclosing characters' words

BANNER — headline running across page

BEAT — reporter's regular assignment; i.e., city hall, police department

BODY TYPE — type used in story, not headline

B.F. (BOLD FACE) — heavy, dark type

BINDER LINE — one headline over a number of related stories

BOX — type bordered by ruled lines

BREAK — where story goes to next page or column

BULLETIN — important last-minute news

BUREAU — news–gathering body or office away from main office

BYLINE — name of writer at top of story

CANNED COPY — news already edited elsewhere and ready to print, such as publicity

CAPS — capital letters

CAPTION — title or description with picture

CIRCULATION — total number of copies of newspaper distributed in one day

CIRCUS MAKEUP — mixture of headline sizes and type faces

CLASSIFIED ADS — advertising space purchased in small amounts by the public

COLUMNIST — writer of special column

COMPOSE — to set in type

COPY — written material to be printed

COPY READER — person who corrects or edits copy written by reporter

or from wire service; may also write headlines

COPYRIGHT — author's or publisher's right to story

COVER — to get material for a story

CREDIT — attribution or identification of source, as for photograph

CRUSADE — program sponsored by paper to arouse public interest

CUB — beginning reporter

CUT — to shorten a story

CUTLINES — information under picture

DATELINE — name of city where story originated, printed at beginning of story

DEADLINE — time at which all copy for an edition must be completed

DISPLAY ADS — large, often illustrated, ads purchased by businesses

DUMMY — diagram showing layout of page

EARS — space on either side of paper's name on front page

EDITOR — person who revises and prepares articles for publication; writes editorials

EDITION — the issue for one press run; e.g., city edition, suburban edition

EDITORIAL — expression of opinion by editor, editorial writer, publisher

EM — measure of type width

EXCLUSIVE — story published by only one paper

EXTRA — before era of radio and TV, a special edition of late news

FEATURE — story where main interest is something other than news value

FILE — to send a story by cable, telegraph, or telephone

FILLER — trivial information to fill space

FIVE Ws — who, what, when, where, why

FOLD — place where paper is folded in half

FOURTH ESTATE — Traditional phrase for the press, originating in the eighteenth century.*

GALLEY — metal tray holding set type

HANDOUT — prepared statement to the press

HEADLINE (HEAD) — kernel sentence at top of story summarizing main points

JUMP — story continued on another page

KILL — to take out a story that was ready to print

L.C. (LOWER CASE) — small letters

LEAD — first paragraph or two of story introducing or summarizing story

LIBEL — publication of information damaging to someone's reputation

LINOTYPE — machine for setting lines of type in hot lead

MAKEUP — layout of stories, pictures, ads in paper

MASTHEAD — information printed in every paper stating title, owner, management, etc.

MORE — another page of copy follows

MORGUE — file of clippings from paper for reference

MUST — label indicating story must be printed

NEWSHOLE — space allotted in newspaper to news as opposed to paid advertising

OBITUARY (OBIT) — brief biography published at time of a person's death

PLAGIARISM — literary theft; passing off as one's own work that of another

PROOF — page of newly set material to be checked for errors before printing

PROOFREADER — one who checks proofs

PUBLICITY — news story about coming events

PUBLISHER — chief business executive, often owner, of newspaper

PUT TO BED — final step before putting paper out, starting presses

RELEASE — (1) print a previously prepared story; (2) publicity prepared by other organizations for use by newspaper

REPORTER — person who collects information and writes news stories

RUNNING STORY — story that continues over a period of time

SCOOP — get a story out to the public before your competitors

SET — put story into type

SLANT — to present only one aspect of a story

SOB STUFF — sentimental stories: dogs, babies

SPOT NEWS — unexpected last–minute news

SPREAD — most important news of the day

STET — let it stand

STYLEBOOK — printed book of guidelines for accepted spelling, punctuation, etc.

SUBHEAD — small-type headlines used to break up long story

---

*During a speech in Parliament, British statesman Edmund Burke pointed to the reporters' gallery, saying, "There are three estates in Parliament, but yonder sits the fourth estate, more important than all of them." He was referring to the three classes of people recognized under British law—the clergy, the nobles, and the commons. Thus, newspapers became the fourth estate.

SYNDICATED FEATURE — material such as columns, comics, etc. purchased from news syndicates

TABLOID — smaller size newspaper with many pictures and short stories

THIRTY (30; ###) — signifies end of copy

TIME COPY — story set in type to be used later

TYPO — typographical error

U.C. (UPPER CASE) — capital letters

UNIFAX — machine that receives and sends wire photos

UPI — United Press International

XV. SPACE FOR YOUR IDEAS

What Is News?

CONTENTS

NEWS VALUES

1. TIMELINESS, IMMEDIACY. What is today's top news? What was last week's? How many remember. . .?

2. PROXIMITY, NEARNESS. Think of examples of local news that would be of no interest outside town; examples of state, regional, or national news.

3. CONSEQUENCE. Think of events that seriously affect the country, your community, yourself as an individual; your family's safety, income; your chances for the future; your personal interests.

4. PROMINENCE. Which will make the front page: how your next-door neighbor spent her vacation or how the president spent his? Think of other examples of prominence besides celebrities (such as national institutions, causes).

5. CONFLICT. Conflict is the basic ingredient of any good story, factual or fictional.* Without it, the reader's first reaction is "So what?" Conflict provides action, suspense; its results are often of great consequence. Think of a few common examples: war, politics, environmental issues, local issues.

6. DRAMA. Drama could be defined as heightened conflict. The very real conflict that goes on daily in the halls of Congress, for example, is not so dramatic as a volcano or a murder, but it may be of greater consequence. Some events are dramatic by their very nature. A good reporter tries to portray these accurately. Capitalizing on the public's eagerness for excitement by overdramatizing ordinary news is a type of inaccurate reporting known as sensationalism.

7. ODDITY, UNUSUALNESS. Even your next-door neighbor will make national headlines if she gives birth to quintuplets.

8. SEX. Any news item that mentions romance, marriage, divorce, women's rights, homosexuality, or related subjects has an unfailing attraction for readers.

9. EMOTIONS. Emotions, such as frustration, fear, hunger, the need for shelter, generosity, courage, sacrifice, satisfaction, are often the subject of human interest features, but can frequently be found in straight news articles as well. Think of examples from the news of the day.

Off Limits

To the *Chronicle:*

Your article on AIDS may be alright in some respects; but if you expect us to favor the spreading of homosexual ideas, as your writer does in his article...forget it.

The Bible teaches normal sex relations between a man and his wife...anything else is sinful...and that is just what that article has done...it is speaking out in favor of sinful sex acts.

From now on, the *Chronicle* will be off-limits to us. We hope that other churches will turn away from all publications that advocate sinful sex.

A Member of C.O.N.

*Cross Reference: Chapter 9, "English": I. Reading, B. Literature

What Is News?

I. DISCOVERING NEWS VALUES

Activities in Chapter 1 have provided a good general picture of newspapers and how they take shape. Now it's time to look more closely at their number one ingredient. Just what **is** news? Before asking your class to supply some answers to this question, you might want to prepare a bulletin board that illustrates some or all of the commonly accepted news values listed opposite, without labeling them, using the board for ACTIVITY 1 below. ACTIVITIES 2 and 3 offer other alternatives. Depending on your assessment of the class's needs, you may either point out that most articles contain more than one news element, or let them discover this for themselves.

ACTIVITIES

1. Allow students to study the unlabeled bulletin board, then ask them, "What is news?" The discussion that follows should develop a list roughly approximating the one opposite. Permitting a reasonable amount of flexibility to include their insights, have students devise their own labels to complete the bulletin board.

2. Do not prepare a bulletin board beforehand. Instead, have students design their own after the opening discussion.

3. After the discussion in which students have developed a list of news values, pass out newspapers and ask them to find examples of each of the news elements, either for class discussion or as a "cut–and–paste" written assignment. When more than one news element is found in an article, students should look for the predominating one to label.

4. Another alternative, perhaps more intellectually challenging, would be to analyze a front page for the news elements represented in its contents. Are they **all** there? Which are most numerous? This would be more fruitful as a class or group discussion project, since students would have a chance to question the value of articles, note that several elements are usually present in a given story, and offer a basis for evaluation and comparison among several papers. If, for example, each group were to examine a different publication, an informal panel discussion could follow where each paper's emphases or biases were presented. As with many exercises in this book, the idea is to heighten critical awareness.

II. SUMMARY LEAD

Examination of several papers for news elements should reveal that the front page of a serious, general interest daily will contain more straight, factual news than human interest features. The latter may either present timely sidelights to the hard news stories or offer a sharp contrast. Editors try to keep their front pages varied and lively. Students may also have noticed that they have only to read a paragraph or two to discover the major news elements in each story. This is because straight news stories usually have what is known as a **summary lead** (an opening that sums up the story). The summary lead first appeared in the late nineteenth century when developing technology poured volumes of news on editors' desks, making it necessary to condense and focus information for publication. (See illustration on next page.)

The first paragraph of a typical news story usually contains the famous "Five Ws"—Who, What, Where, When, Why—and an H—How. Why and How may require further explanation, and may sometimes be found in the second or third paragraph. The straight summary lead is not the only way to begin a story. Other types of leads, which will be discussed in Chapter 3, "Features: The Other Kind of News," essentially contain the Five Ws, though they are not always so obvious. (See Example C, page 32.)

ACTIVITIES

5. Using the daily paper, assign each story on the front page to an individual, row, or group of students, depending on size of class and number of stories. Have them find the Five Ws for each story. Discuss these briefly.*

6. Have students analyze headlines to see which of the Five Ws are used as a basis for the headline. How well does the headline sum up the story's content? (Headlines will be given further attention in this chapter.)

III. INVERTED PYRAMID

As we discovered when we glanced through the daily paper, we don't usually read a story all the way through unless we are unusually interested in the topic or, perhaps, the writer has cleverly captured our interest. Still, we know what happened, the story's climax, just from reading the first paragraph. The details follow in descending order of importance, in what is known as the "inverted pyramid" style. You wouldn't want to read a detective story or a romance constructed this way, but it serves two important purposes in a news story. The reader can read only as much as desired and still know the

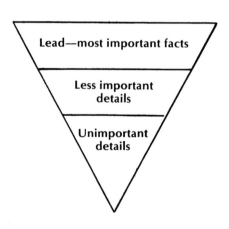

Lead—most important facts

Less important details

Unimportant details

---

*Cross Reference: See Chapter 9, "English": III. Writing, B. Grammar, for an exercise using the five Ws to explain sentence structure.

A CLASSIC ACCOUNT OF BULL RUN*

New York Herald, July 20 and 29, 1001.

CENTERVILLE, SIX AND A HALF MILES FROM MANASSAS JUNCTION, THURSDAY, JULY 18, 5 P.M.—I have just returned from the thickest of an action of considerable moment, between a portion of the rebel forces and the Fourth Brigade of General Tyler's division, composed of the Second and Third Michigan, the First Massachusetts, and Twelfth New York Volunteer regiments, under command of Colonel Richardson; and as the aide of General McDowell, who will carry the official report of the affair to General Scott, and who offers the only means of communication with Washington this evening, is about starting, I have only time to send you the following brief particular of today's operation.

At eleven o'clock General Tyler proceeded to make a reconnaissance in force, with Captain Ayres' (late Sherman's) battery, four companies of cavalry, and Colonel Richardson's brigade, composed as above stated. Advancing up the road to Bull's Run for about two miles, the column came to an opening, after passing through a long stretch of timber, when sight was caught of a strong body of the enemy. General Tyler immediately ordered Captain Ayres' battery to advance and open on them, which they did from a commanding elevation. Eight shells had been thrown, when suddenly a volley was fired upon us from a hidden battery, about a mile down the road.

Our howitzers then threw some grapeshot into the timber, when at once a terrific series of volleys of musketry was poured out from the woods upon the troops outside. At the same time a battery commenced playing upon us from an elevation in the rear. Shot of every description flew about us like hail; but it being, fortunately, nearly all aimed too high, hardly anyone was struck outside the woods.

A retreat was now ordered, when infantry, cavalry, and artillery fell back behind our battery on the hill. The Twelfth New York and a portion of the First Massachusetts broke ranks and scattered in different directions, in their hasty retreat, for some distance through the woods, in the rear of the battery.

Our troops fought under great disadvantage. Not one rebel ventured out of the woods during the action. *The affair was not an attack, but merely a reconnaissance* to discover the position and strength of the enemy.

This story, by Henry Villard of the *New York Herald,* is typical of the narrative style of journalism that prevailed in earlier times.

*Reprinted by permission of John Wiley and Sons, Inc., New York, copyright 1984, from *Voices of the Past* by Calder M. Pickett, Columbus, Ohio, Grid, Inc., 1977.

THE FIVE Ws

Example A

PLO defends last base

TRIPOLI, Lebanon (AP) — Yasser Arafat and his PLO fighters, driven from one refugee camp under intense artillery fire, regrouped Sunday to defend their last Middle East stronghold against a tank-led assault by Syrian-backed mutineers.

Cohen plays key role in freeze fight

IBM model may reshape home market

NEW YORK (AP) — IBM finally lifted the veil Tuesday from its much-anticipated home computer, the PCjr — a machine expected to reshape the $2 billion market by raising the complexity and price of home computers.

Example B.

By KENDALL HOLMES
Guy Gannett Service

WASHINGTON — It was a heady night, albeit one filled with a somewhat ambiguous victory, for Republican Sen. William S. Cohen.

As the U.S. Senate slogged through a proposal Monday to increase the nation's debt limit, leaders of the nuclear freeze movement successfully forced the first Senate vote ever on the freeze.

Cohen led the floor debate against the freeze — and when a vote came hours later, the Senate voted 58-40 to table the freeze. Next, Cohen forced the Senate to consider for the first time the nuclear weapons build-down proposal he and others favor as an alternative to the freeze.

Example C

Finding the Five Ws is not always as easy as it sounds. Example A is quite straightforward.

    Where: Tripoli, Lebanon
    Who: Yasser Arafat and his PLO fighters
    What: regrouped
    How: under intense artillery fire
    When: Sunday
    Why: to defend their stronghold

Example B is also relatively simple.

    Where: New York
    Who: IBM
    What: lifted the veil
    When: Sunday
    Why and How: not given

But Example C is more complex. The lead material is spread over three paragraphs, adding variety and color, while still providing the basic information.

    Where: Washington
    Who: Senator William S. Cohen (and nuclear freeze leaders)
    What: led the floor debate
    When: Monday
    How: successfully

And these choices might be argued. Note how the headline sums up the lead in each of the stories.

essentials, and the editor, trying to fit all the important happenings of the day into the paper, can cut the story from the bottom up without losing the most important facts and especially, when time is of the essence, without having to rearrange them to make sense. A good reporter quickly learns to write this way. It's not so easy as one might think without trying it. Exercises to illustrate this point, however, are not hard to devise. Several, which also serve to sharpen any student's discrimination between major and minor details, follow.

ACTIVITIES

7. Select a news story of five to seven paragraphs that clearly illustrates this descending order of importance. Make a copy of the original, then cut it apart and paste it up in jumbled order. Provide a copy of the jumbled story for each student. (This is easy to tailor to any ability level.) After students have reconstructed the story, project or pass out copies of the original. Encourage discerning comment from any who disagree with the order. It's likely that a different ordering of details can be defended.

8. Ask students to find examples of news stories that to them seem **not** written in diminishing order of importance. Have them defend their criticism in either a brief oral statement or a one-paragraph critique.[1]

9. Have students find the same story in several different papers and look for different choices in the order of importance as well as different emphases in the headlines. Discuss how this changes the effect of the story on the reader and why it might have been done. Reasons could include the professionalism of the newspaper staff, the political outlook of the publisher, the paper's accepted style, the audience it's aimed at, or just simple desperation. Copy editors are required to keep up a killing pace and occasionally miss an obvious point. Ask students if this exercise tells them anything about objectivity in journalism.

10. Provide students with a short story written in narrative style and ask them to rewrite it in inverted pyramid style. This kind of drill is useful not only in understanding the newspaper, but also in learning to organize material for any kind of writing.[2]

11. Have students write a news story of five or six paragraphs in inverted pyramid style about a recent school event. (Stress timelines here.)

IV. WRITING A NEWS STORY

Although students have been reading (and more or less listening to) the "inverted pyramid" in news presentations for years, having to write in a style other than the "beginning-middle-end" essay form they have been taught might cause some initial distress. They will take heart when you remind them (and provide them with specific examples from the daily paper) that newspaper paragraphs are very short, indeed, are often only one or two sentences. News writing is direct, crisp, and simple and avoids the complex sentence structures

---

[1]**Cross Reference:** Chapter 9, "English": I. Reading, A. Comprehension; III. Writing, A. Composition

[2]*Ibid.*

more appropriate to exposition. How to avoid the expression of personal opinion in news writing is often difficult for students to grasp. They have the greatest problem when writing about conflict in their own bailiwick: rival sports teams, unpopular administrative policies, controversial courses, the food in the cafeteria. While this is not intended as a journalism text, the need to understand the often subtle distinction between fact and opinion is so universal that a teacher does well to use any means of getting at it from a fresh perspective.[1] How opinion is appropriately expressed in the newspaper will be treated more fully in Chapter 4, "The Editorial Pages: Matter of Opinion." For our purposes, sufficient examples of difficulty with fact and opinion should appear in the students' own news stories to provide ample illustration.

ACTIVITY

12. Select several such examples and provide copies for the class. Work together to find ways of expressing "opinions" as "facts." The following example might serve as a model.

Example:

Central High Student Government discussed circulating a petition to get rid of the rotten food in the cafeteria at their last meeting. The principal, Mr. Jones, is going to look into the problem.

In whose opinion is the food rotten? The newspaper can express no opinion except on the editorial page. The writer cannot express his own opinion, even if he has a byline, unless he is writing a review. Did the principal actually say he would look into it? If so, it should be in the form of a quotation, direct or indirect. If the reporter merely inferred it, he shouldn't have.

Revision:

A petition requesting a change in the cafeteria menu was drafted at last week's meeting of Central High Student Government in response to numerous complaints collected in a recent *Crier* survey.

"It's rotten," said a senior boy. (Senior class president John Parker)

"Pea soup every Wednesday is too much," a sophomore girl (Judy Brown) complained. "Why can't we have hot dogs and pizza more than once a month?"

"Constructive suggestions from students will be given due consideration," Principal Harold T. Jones told the *Crier*.

Depending on the atmosphere in a given school, students could be personally identified, as indicated in parentheses. Merely attributing the opinions to someone, however, is sufficient. The ethical implications of using unidentified sources in professional journalism are complex.[2]

---

[1] Insights into the semantic complexities of fact vs. opinion may be gained from S.I. Hayakawa's widely-read *Language in Thought and Action* (New York: Harcourt, Brace and World, Inc., 1964), Chapter 3, "Reports, Inferences, Judgments."

[2] **Cross Reference:** Chapters 7, 8, and 11 discuss freedom of the press.

In straight news writing, the general rule is that any opinion expressed in a story must be **attributed** to a source, usually an identified speaker, who is quoted directly or indirectly. A crime is "alleged" to have been committed by a "suspect," who may become "the accused" (innocent until proven guilty), and after due process, a "convicted" criminal (the court's opinion, not that of Divine Justice, thus leaving open the possibility of later exoneration). Engagements are "announced" by the parties involved or their parents. Carelessness on this point has led to more than one libel suit. How news is collected from various sources is detailed in Chapter 3, "Features: The Other Kind of News": III. How to Write Features, and ACTIVITIES 9–12.

V. HEADLINES

A newspaper headline is not a title, such as "Red Sox Game" or "Star Wars," but a summary of the story that follows. Quite often it is a condensation of the lead paragraph. Properly, a headline is a kernel sentence, containing a subject and a verb, without auxiliaries, pronouns, articles, or conjunctions.*

House panel revives amendment

Example A. A headline is a simple sentence.

China keeping
Hong Kong deadline

Example B. The auxiliary "is" is rarely used in a headline; it is understood.

U.S., Soviets
hold more talks

Example C. A comma takes the place of "and" in headlines.

Day's sells building;
store to be restored

Example D. A semicolon separates two "sentences."

Pope urges peace
in Lebanon

Example E. A prepositional phrase is never split between two lines.

These rules are frequently violated, occasionally for good reasons, such as stylistic variations in feature material, where titles (of regular columns, for example) are appropriate. Editorials also use titles quite regularly. But for news stories, respected papers observe the headline rules carefully. Clarity and accurate reflection of the story underneath are even

*Cross Reference: Chapter 9, "English": III. Writing, B. Grammar

more important than strict adherence to rules. Confusing, inappropriate, and sometimes humorously embarrassing headlines do occur. (See example below.) Writing headlines can help to increase reading accuracy and comprehension and develop the ability to find the central theme.

Blind Institution Director Hopes To Clear Critical Air

The director of the Maine Institution for the Blind hopes to clear the air today of charges that the Portland-based agency has strayed from its original purpose and plunged itself into finincial difficulties.

Fxample F. **Confusing headline**

ACTIVITY

13. Provide students with copies of one or more articles from which headlines have been removed and ask them to write headlines for them. Then supply the original headlines for comparison.

One reason headlines sometimes seem farfetched is the problem of fitting the best words into limited space using large type. As linguists have observed, there is no **exact** synonym for any word in the language, and a near substitute that fits the space may miss by a mile.

ACTIVITY

14. Select several news stories with headlines attached. Have students rewrite the headlines substituting synonyms for key words. Discuss whether their substitutions summarize the story more or less accurately than the original. Could the change in any way alter the reader's perception of the story? Ask them to find synonyms that would clearly change the story's impact.* Would the synonyms chosen fit in the same space?

When a copy reader receives a story to edit, instructions for the size and type of headline to be written come with it, for example: 18-point, two-line, one-column head.

*Cross Reference: Chapter 9, "English": II. Language, A. Semantics

NEWSPAPER TYPE

Type is measured in points. Point size refers to the height of the letter. Lines of type are measured in picas, approximately six picas to the inch. The larger the point size of the type, the fewer letters will fit a given column width of, for example, 13 picas. This paragraph is printed in 11-point Chelmsford. Chelmsford is the name of the type design. The lines are 31 picas wide. The text of this book is printed in 11-point Times Modern, in lines of 33 picas. The activities are in 11-point Times Modern, 31 picas wide.

Newspapers use a variety of page sizes and column widths. Headlines are most often 18, 24, 30, 36, 48, and 72 points in size. The sample sizes below were printed in boldface Times Modern.

18-point

24-point

30-point

36-point

48-point

72-point

© 1985 J. Weston Walch, Publisher

Modern computers count the number of picas in a headline as fast as it can be composed on the VDT screen. The writer knows at once whether it will fit. Coming up with the right words, however, still depends on the human brain. Before the computer era, the rough rule of thumb for "counting" heads was *m*'s and *w*'s count two; *l*'s, *i*'s, and punctuation (except question marks) count one half; all other lower-case (small) letters and spaces between the words count one. Count for upper-case (capital) letters varies with the type face, but is roughly one and a half for most letters, two and a half for *M*'s and *W*'s, and one for *I*'s.

ACTIVITY

15. Provide students with copies of several news stories, headlines removed. Ask them to write a one-column, two-line (24-point) headline with a count of 12 and a two-column, two-line headline (36 point) with a count of 15. (The two-column head, being larger type size, would not have twice the count as the one-column head.) Let them work in teams or groups. In the struggle to find the elusive right word for the right space, colleagues in newsrooms are often called upon for help. This exercise will not only sharpen vocabulary skills,* but also foster an awareness of the work that goes into a newspaper.

VI. LAYOUT

Why write one-column, two-column, and larger headlines in various type sizes anyway? Students will probably come up with the commonsense answer that it has to do with the appearance of the paper and the relative importance of the many stories. What may not be so apparent is that this arrangement has a name: LAYOUT. Literally, how the pages are laid out. The examination of the front page (Chapter 1, ACTIVITIES 9, 10, and 24) covered many of the essentials of layout. Graphic design will be considered briefly in Chapter 10, "The Arts": III. Visual Arts, A. Graphics and Design. Both the aesthetic theories and the mechanical practices of newspaper graphics are vast and intriguing fields which some students may wish to investigate further. Chapter 15, "Career Education," will touch briefly on these possibilities, too. The purpose here is to bring its existence to their attention and to examine some of its basic features.

ACTIVITY

16. Hang up across the front of the room a variety of newspaper front pages, standard and tabloid, from the classroom collection. Ask students to observe how different arrangements of pictures, headlines, type styles, and stories give each paper its own personality. Which ones do they find most attractive? Why?

Important visual considerations are variety, contrast, and balance. These are achieved by thoughtful arrangement of text or "body" material, heavier headlines, pictures, and white space. Some papers, like the *New York Times*, seldom vary in their daily appearance. Others develop more imaginative approaches which can range from tasteful to downright garish. Editors try to avoid "gray" areas of type by breaking up long stories with boldface

*Cross Reference: Chapter 9, "English": III. Writing, C. Vocabulary

boxes and subheads; top- or bottom-heaviness of black type or pictures; and tombstones, two headlines side by side that can be read as one (nonsensically).

There are endless type styles from which to choose for headlines, but most newspapers stick to one or two easily readable faces. Point sizes from 14 to 72, augmented by italic, boldface, condensed, and outline variants, offer endless possibilities. Students may notice the contrasting effect of serif faces used by many papers to sans serif faces seen in others. (See page 40 for examples.)

The initial impact of the front page is vital in creating a newspaper's image, but layout does not end there. Other pages have their characteristic layouts, quickly identified by regular readers: political cartoons on the editorial page, imaginative art work in the feature section, informality in the sports headlines, fine-print columns on the financial pages, and advertising competing for space with news (though almost never on the front page or the editorial pages) To give students a little familiarity with the concept of layout and to help summarize this chapter, the following activity offers a taste of hands-on experience.*

VII. DESIGNING A FRONT PAGE

ACTIVITY

17. Divide the class into groups of three or four. Make this a one-period project to emphasize the ever-present deadline that affects the character of the daily paper. Provide each group with a sketch pad, an assortment of articles and pictures clipped from newspapers, and page-size newsprint for use as a dummy. (Editors responsible for the layout of various newspaper pages usually sketch a rough idea for their layout, then plan it accurately on a page-size sheet called a "dummy." The final page to be printed is put together according to the dummy, following the method appropriate to the printing technique involved.) The task in this activity is to design a **front page** and lay out the articles and pictures to fit the space. Room must be left for the flag, headlines, pictures, picture captions, and other components of the front page. (See Chapter 1, ACTIVITY 10.) Stories may be cut or deleted, judiciously, of course. Headlines must be written. They will probably want to invent a name for this fictional paper, but it is likely to be too time consuming, so don't encourage it. The following day, display the front pages. Have students discuss the problems they encountered and the rules (as in headline writing) they may have failed to observe. If you decide to ask for written critiques following the discussion, have students evaluate their own projects.

VIII. CHAPTER EVALUATION

Many of the activities in this chapter can be used as written assignments, projects, or tests for purposes of evaluation. The matching objective quiz that follows may be photocopied.

---

*Cross Reference: Another, more involved, layout activity can be found in Chapter 7, "Newspaper and History": II. Newspaper in History Project.

TYPE FACES

Giants, Cards in tie

Example A. Serif type face

A study in speculation illustrates a life

Example B. Sans serif type face

Raid hit 'thugs,' Reagan explains

WASHINGTON (AP) — President Reagan said Tuesday U.S. and Caribbean troops invaded Grenada to protect 1,000 Americans and restore democracy to a nation run by "a brutal group of leftist thugs."

Two U.S. soldiers were killed and the invaders encountered greater resistance than expected from Cuban and Grenadian defenders, U.S. officials said.

Meanwhile congressional reaction to the invasion was mixed. Some members of Congress welcomed the move. Others assailed the new military venture.

✔ **The initial invasion was carried out entirely by U.S. Marines and Army Rangers. Page 2.**

✔ **Planners of the invasion anticipated protests. Page 11**

✔ **The desicion to invade apparently was made last week. Page 2**

✔ **A Maine ham radio operator monitored the action. Page 2.**

Example C. News headline and part of story, showing use of boldface for emphasis.

U.S. reassures Soviet Union

82nd Airborne joins U.S. forces in Grenada

Example D. News headline with italic kicker

Example E (left). Outline type face

Name _____ Date _____

OBJECTIVE QUIZ: TERMS

In the blank before each item in Column A, write the letter of the description in Column B that best fits it.

A	**B**
____ 1. Dummy	a. Type face with short finishing strokes at the ends of letters
____ 2. Point	b. Widely known
____ 3. Pica	c. The time when the paper must be ready for printing
____ 4. Sensationalism	d. Timeliness, being up-to-the-minute
____ 5. Summary lead	e. Something that can be proved by observation
____ 6. Inverted pyramid	f. Full-size plan indicating location of all material on a newspaper page
____ 7. Tombstone	g. Newswriting style in which information is given in descending order of importance
____ 8. Deadline	h. The clash of opposing forces or ideas
____ 9. Serif	i. Opening paragraph that sums up a story
____ 10. Sans serif	j. Said to be, so-called
____ 11. Italic	k. Necessary information in a news story
____ 12. Immediacy	l. Overdramatization of a news event
____ 13. Proximity	m. Type face with smooth letter strokes
____ 14. Consequence	n. Unit of measure for length of a printed line
____ 15. Prominence	o. Slanted type face
____ 16. Conflict	p. A belief, judgment, or guess
____ 17. Five Ws	q. Nearness
____ 18. Fact	r. Two headlines side by side that could be read as one
____ 19. Opinion	s. Unit of measure for type size
____ 20. Alleged	t. Having an important outcome

ANSWERS TO
—————— OBJECTIVE QUIZ: TERMS ——————

1. f	11. o
2. s	12. d
3. n	13. q
4. l	14. t
5. i	15. b
6. g	16. h
7. r	17. k
8. c	18. e
9. a	19. p
10. m	20. j

IX. SPACE FOR YOUR IDEAS

Features:
The Other Kind of News

CONTENTS

Features: The Other Kind of News

I. IDENTIFYING FEATURES

Straight, serious, unembellished information, as important as it is, represents only a fraction of the content of a newspaper. The trend toward more extensive and varied feature material has been gaining momentum as people rely increasingly on the instant electronic media for coverage of spot news. In order to survive, newspapers must try to offer things the public can get nowhere else. Features could loosely be described as all the stories in the paper that are not hard news: human interest, vacation, travel, entertainment, history, natural science, seasonal and holiday material, as well as regularly appearing columns. Feature articles often differ from news articles not so much in their topics as in their approach. An event in the daily spot news frequently generates a spinoff of satellite features that orbits around the original subject: personality profiles of leading characters, background stories, indepth analysis by recognized experts. Features can vary from highly informative or soundly entertaining to sensational or merely decorative, depending on the nature of the publication. Among their distinguishing characteristics are:

1. An attention-getting headline.

2. A lead designed to capture the reader's interest through such approaches as suspense, direct appeal (often a question), quotations, description of setting, mood or personality, or other clever devices, provided they are not gimmicky.

3. More informal or colorful language than is found in straight news stories, often displaying a writer's individual style.

4. An essay structure rather than the inverted pyramid. In order to work toward an effective climax, a good feature should be tailored to the length the editor has assigned and tightly constructed to hold the reader's attention to the end. For this reason, it is difficult to cut, which is why feature stories often appear on inside pages or special sections that are not printed at the last minute, allowing time for editing.

5. Expression of opinion by individual writers of analysis, reviews and regular columns, syndicated or of local origin.

6. Subject matter of perennial interest that is not soon outdated, so that it may be used whenever space permits. Newspapers keep such stories "standing" (as they used to say of metal type that was already set, in the "bank") or, in more modern terminology, on file in the computer bank, where they can be retrieved at the touch of a button.

A good way for students to get acquainted with various types of features is to send them, in teams of two or three, on a scavenger hunt.

ACTIVITIES

1. Here is a suggested list for a feature story scavenger hunt. Amend or adapt it to your needs. Nothing is cut and dried. Some lively discussion is likely to follow the hunt.

   - News feature directly related to a hard news article in the same paper

   - News feature of current interest but not limited to a brief moment in time

   - Human interest "tie-in" indirectly related to news of the day

   - Human interest story with no time limit (children, animals, unusual hobbies are good examples)

   - Seasonal mood piece

   - Seasonal article related to outdoor recreation or travel

   - Single feature intended primarily as information (how-to in the kitchen, home, or workshop, for example)

   - Family-type humorous column, local

   - Family-type humorous column, syndicated, such as Erma Bombeck

   - "Serious" syndicated column on health, beauty, love life, bridge, chess, etc.

   - Profile of an interesting personality, local or otherwise

   - Review of a movie, book, or live performance

   - Feature story on the arts

2. A slightly different scavenger hunt could seek features with:

   - A suspenseful lead

   - A particularly provocative headline

   - A lead that asks a question

   - A lead that begins with a direct quotation

   - A lead that sets a specific mood

   - An especially unusual approach to the subject

It should be pointed out that straight news stories also use these devices in their leads, rather than sticking solely to the so-called "clothesline" lead that hangs the five Ws in a straight row. But features are still easily recognized by their other characteristics.

ACTIVITIES

3. Have students find a straight news article and a feature article directly related to it. They should list facts found in both articles and discuss differences in the language used to present the same information, list facts found only in the news article and discuss why, list facts found only in the feature article and discuss why. Finally, they should discuss what they may have gained by reading both articles, rather than one or the other.

4. As an in-class written assignment, have each student choose the article in the day's paper that he or she enjoyed the most and write a short paragraph explaining why, using newspaper terminology wherever possible. ("Enjoy" should not necessarily imply entertainment. A student might easily prefer a serious informative article.)

5. As an alternative, students might be asked to find a feature article presenting information of special interest or use to themselves and explain how they can use the information.

II. FINDING COLORFUL WORDS

Many a general assignment reporter covering city council and sewer district meetings longs for the opportunity to write colorful, in-depth feature articles that will give scope to the hidden talent that may one day uncover another Watergate or produce the great American novel. Though the same journalistic discipline that demands accurate, responsible reporting of hard news applies equally to the writing of non-fiction articles, these do allow a greater range of vocabulary and imagery. The best writing of any kind requires the selection of exactly the right word to convey the meaning of a fact or idea. It has often been said that concrete nouns and active verbs, rather than descriptive adjectives and adverbs, are the essence of good writing.*

ACTIVITIES

6. Have students select a feature story from the daily paper and list all the nouns and verbs. As a class, analyze each one for the amount of information it conveys on its own. Ask students which nouns and verbs are most effective in the story. Have them suggest meatier substitutes for the weaker ones.

7. Using the same story or another, list nouns and verbs with their modifiers (if any). Ask whether the modifiers contribute to the meaning of the story or slow down the pace. How could they be eliminated by using more informative nouns and verbs? Are there some nouns and verbs in the story that would benefit from modifiers? Ask for suggestions.

*Cross Reference: Chapter 9, "English": III. Writing, C. Vocabulary

An important consideration to bear in mind in the preceding activities is the matter of bias and opinion, already discussed in connection with objectivity (Chapter 1, ACTIVITIES 17, 18) and with headline writing (Chapter 2, ACTIVITY 14).

ACTIVITY

8. Have students examine the nouns and verbs they have listed and substituted in ACTIVITIES 6 and 7 (page 49) to make sure that they are essentially descriptive or informative, and do not carry any judgmental connotation.[1]

III. HOW TO WRITE FEATURES

Identifying feature stories and analyzing their style is one thing. Writing them is another matter. The same basic approach applies to all non-fiction writing: news, feature, and research. Background material may be collected from the reference library and clipping file (known as the "morgue") that every good newspaper maintains, as well as from public and university libraries and the public information services of business, government, and cultural institutions. A good reporter keeps eyes and ears open and develops a "nose for news," as well as a long list of "contacts," people who know what's going on inside the reporter's field of interest. The best place to go for information is the source—the key person in a situation, on the scene where it's happening. Firsthand information is usually the best. Knowing how to conduct an effective interview is essential to getting this information, whether it's for a news story or a feature. The feature interview may be more leisurely and informal, where the news interview is efficient and concise, but the basics remain the same. A list of steps for a successful interview on the following page may be reproduced.[2]

ACTIVITY

9. Practice interviewing in class, using a tape recorder or, even better, a videotape camera, if either is available. If not, this is a good opportunity to practice note-taking. The rest of the class should be taking notes in any case. Select a public official or personality, local or national, and an appropriate issue or topic for an interview with him or her. A student or the teacher can play the role of interviewee. One or more students can practice interviewing, making the necessary preparations and following the steps listed on the handout sheet. After the interview, have the class discuss the manner in which it was conducted.

   – Was the reporter courteous and businesslike?

   – Did he or she get all the essential information?

   Other class members might list anything that was forgotten.

---

[1]**Cross Reference:** Chapter 9, "English": II. Language, A. Semantics
[2]**Cross Reference:** Showing copy to interviewee—Chapter 8, "The Newspaper Today": III. Libel, V. Right to Know

IV. STEPS FOR A SUCCESSFUL INTERVIEW

1. Begin with a phone call to set up an appointment at the subject's convenience.

2. Before the time agreed on, do your homework. Go to the morgue and other sources for background on the subject and/or person being interviewed. This will furnish insight into the situation, prevent your embarrassing yourself by asking about things that are common knowledge, and get you more directly to the heart of the topic you are writing about.

3. Develop a list of questions to be answered, keeping them focused on the specific area to be covered in the story.

4. For the interview itself, dress neatly, be prompt, courteous, intelligently curious but not pushy. Be firm, however, about getting the necessary information. Try different approaches if necessary. The direct question is preferable, but you may need to put your subject at ease by talking about his or her interests, hobbies, or accomplishments, or even the weather. Be sure to follow up any new leads that come up. You may find the real story is different from the one you came for.

5. **Most important of all:** Take accurate notes. Don't be afraid to ask the person to repeat or explain technical information, figures, or anything you're not sure you heard correctly. Be sure to ask for his or her official title and the correct spelling of his or her name. Jot down the color of eyes and hair, facial expressions, habitual gestures, details of clothing and surroundings, decor, furniture, weather—anything that will lend concrete images to create a clearer, more interesting picture for the reader. Absorb the mood and observe the background of the situation. You may never need this information, but it's hard to go back for when you're in the middle of writing and suddenly realize that it would add a great deal to your story.

6. If you use a tape recorder, practice first to discover the best position (distance may be crucial) for getting necessary clarity. Some hand-held microphones can be pointed toward the speaker, then back to yourself to record the questions. Some are very sensitive and need to be placed in a central location and not touched while recording.

7. Be sure to thank the person you interview. You may be asked to show him or her a copy of the story before it is published. Explain that this is not customary journalistic practice. (As a "professional," it is your job to get the facts straight and present them fairly. In agreeing to talk to you, the subject has tacitly acknowledged this.) It is fair for him or her to ask that certain remarks be "off the record"—that is, not to be published—during the interview, which you should agree to unless they are the whole story! Offer to double-check any sensitive details for accuracy before publication, but don't be pushed into a pre-publication review.

8. Transcribe your notes as soon as you get home while you can still remember what the things you can't decipher mean.

ACTIVITIES

10. Invite an interesting local person to class. The entire class should contribute to research and preparation of questions beforehand. Let the class select one member to interview the guest. This reporter, as well as the rest of the class, takes notes. Every member of the class is required to write a story based on the interview, but only the interviewer should ask questions during it. Encourage students to take different approaches to the story, as listed in ACTIVITY 2, page 48. After they have completed the assignment, discuss the interview.

11. Invite a local official to class for a news conference on a matter of current controversy. Different students should represent different interests in the community and different publications. (Use regional or national ones to represent different points of view if local ones are nonexistent.) In this case both "news" and "feature" reporters should participate. Students may choose their approaches, but must be sure to stick to them when writing their story.

12. Have the teacher, a class member, or another faculty member represent a public personality, and conduct a mock interview or press conference as outlined above.

13. Assign students human interest features of approximately three pages, for which they must do background research and an interview. Stress not only the importance of an out-of-the-ordinary topic, a provocative lead, and a story that will involve the reader to the end, but also accuracy and the absence of the reporter's opinions and/or judgments.

V. REVIEWS

There **is** a place for opinion in feature writing: the review. Film, television, music, art, theater, dance, and books are reviewed regularly in the press.* Expert and amateur writers alike react variously to the same work, sometimes to the detriment of a fine presentation, sometimes to the glorification of a questionable performance, but usually with fairness according to their lights. Students should be reminded that critics are only human, that one man's meat is another man's poison. No one should refrain from attending a performance, watching a program, or reading a book because of a bad review.

ACTIVITIES

14. Have students find reviews of the same work or performance in two or more publications to compare in a class discussion. If possible, divide the class into groups, assigning film, theater, TV, music, art, and book reviews to separate groups. Note the various approaches to reviewing and the sometimes sharply differing opinions.

*Cross Reference: Chapter 10, "The Arts"; Chapter 9, "English": I. Reading, B. Literature

15. Have students find a review or several reviews of a TV program they themselves have seen and compare their impressions with those of the reviewers. This may be an oral or a written assignment.

16. If possible, have students write a brief review of a local dramatic production (preferably **not** a school play, where performers are too likely to be friends—or enemies), a musical or dance performance, or a movie that's playing at a local theater. If all else fails, they can review a TV special currently airing (rather than a regular series, so it will be a fresh experience). The guidelines on the following page are helpful to student reviewers.

Analysis by experts in their fields is another type of feature writing where opinions— usually the kind based on observation of facts rather than moral judgments—are expressed. ACTIVITIES related to these in individual fields can be found in Chapter 5, "Sports, Comics, and Other Special Features"; and in all chapters in Part II.

See page 54, a reproducible page, for helpful tips concerning reviews.

VII. CHAPTER EVALUATION

Many of the activities in this chapter will measure students' understanding of feature material for purposes of evaluation. In addition, an objective quiz with one short essay question, which may be photocopied, follows on page 55.

VI. HINTS FOR REVIEWING PERFORMANCES

1. **Techniques for watching:** Listen and watch carefully, trying to remember details. Jot them down on a note pad or on your program; you can learn to see in the dark. But don't let this keep you from being caught up in the dramatic force of the performance. Your responsiveness is the key to the review.

2. **How to get started writing:** Ask yourself the following questions, then organize your review around the opinions your answers express. *Do not* include the questions or the direct answers in your review, but only the ideas they gave you. You will not need to use all of them, but some will help you get started in the right direction.

   - How was the presentation staged? (simply, elaborately, realistically, abstractly)

   - What equipment—properties, sets, film or video techniques—were used to create setting, mood, atmosphere, expectation?

   - How much was left to your imagination? Was this effective or ineffective?

   - What specific things did the performers do to add to the mood, tension, build-up, climax? How did they make the characters seem real? Should they have seemed real? (Disregard characters when reviewing music—usually!)

   - Which scene or number did you like best? Why?

   - Which scene or number did you like least? Why?

   - Which character or performer did you like best? Why? Were you supposed to?

   - Which character or performer did you like least? Why? Were you supposed to?

   - What was the general theme of the performance? (celebration, despair, reality, fantasy? person vs. person; person vs. God; person vs. society; person vs. himself or herself)

   - What emotions or thoughts did the performance inspire in you? (horror, pity, awe, excitement, boredom, revulsion, sympathy, happiness, sorrow)

3. **Now:** Select the answer to the above questions that you think is the most interesting or important reaction to the performance as a whole, and build your review around it. Make your lead paragraph intriguing enough to involve and perhaps challenge the reader. Supply your opening statement with specific details, such as visual images and/or an opinion, to let the reader know what you think of the performance. Use as many answers to the remaining questions as are appropriate to develop the central section of your review. Finish with a summary of your reaction to the performance.

Name _____ Date _____

_____ QUIZ: FEATURES _____

I. *Put a check mark in the blank beside the choice that best completes the sentence.*

1. Feature articles can be found

    A. ___ only on the front page.

    B. ___ only in the second section.

    C. ___ anywhere in the paper.

    D. ___ only in the Sunday paper.

2. Feature articles are *most* different from news articles in

    A. ___ the way they are written.

    B. ___ their seriousness.

    C. ___ their length.

    D. ___ their subject matter.

3. A feature article is *usually*

    A. ___ about something that happened yesterday.

    B. ___ about children or animals.

    C. ___ written in essay style with a beginning, a middle, and an end.

    D. ___ written in inverted pyramid style.

4. Which of the following is probably *not* a feature article?

    A. ___ An analysis of the United Nations policy on Lebanon.

    B. ___ An obituary.

    C. ___ A movie review.

    D. ___ A personality profile.

5. Which of the following is *not* a common characteristic of feature articles?

    A. ___ An attention-getting headline.

    B. ___ Description.

    C. ___ A clothesline lead.

    D. ___ Informal or colorful language.   *(continued)*

Name _____ Date _____

_____ QUIZ: FEATURES _____
(continued)

II. TRUE–FALSE

T ___ F ___   1. It isn't as important for feature writers to be accurate as it is for news writers.

T ___ F ___   2. Both feature writers and news writers often do research before writing a story.

T ___ F ___   3. The best kind of information is first-hand information.

T ___ F ___   4. You should never ask the person you are interviewing the same question twice.

T ___ F ___   5. Reporters often show stories to their sources before they are published.

III. SHORT ESSAY

Describe the steps you would take to prepare for writing a story on the new director of recreation your town has just appointed. (Do **not** write the story.)

© 1985 J. Weston Walch, Publisher

ANSWERS TO
QUIZ: FEATURES

I. 1. C
   2. A
   3. C (*Usually* is the key word—others are occasional.)
   4. B
   5. C (*Common* is the key word. It *could* happen.)

II. TRUE–FALSE
   1. F
   2. T
   3. T
   4. F (It's less embarrassing to check than to be wrong.)
   5. F (*Often* is the key word.)

III. SHORT ESSAY *(This could be answered in narrative style. Reasonable answers can be accepted.)*
   1. Call and make an appointment to see him.
   2. Look him up in the newspaper files. He may not be there if he's from out of town.
   3. Call the town manager or chairperson of the recreation committee, and ask why the new director was chosen. Ask if they have any information on his background that you could pick up. This doesn't have to be an interview, but take careful notes on what your contact tells you.
   4. Look over the information you have gathered and decide what questions you are going to ask in the interview.
   5. Dress neatly, take your pencil and stenographer's pad and/or tape recorder, and arrive at the appointment just a minute before the time agreed on.
   6. Be friendly and courteous, but keep the questions you want answered in mind. Write down all important details.
   7. Don't be afraid to ask again for points you've missed. Be sure to ask about correct spelling of names.
   8. Follow up any new leads that come into the conversation. You may find you have a different, even better, story.
   9. Don't forget to thank the interviewee as you leave.
   10. Transcribe your notes as soon as you get home, while you still remember what the things you can't decipher mean.

VIII. SPACE FOR YOUR IDEAS

CHAPTER 4

The Editorial Pages:
Matter of Opinion

CONTENTS

The Editorial Pages: Matter of Opinion

I. WHOSE OPINIONS?

The words "editorial" and "opinion" are so closely linked that inappropriate expression of opinion in what is supposed to be factual reporting is called "editorializing." In news stories, opinion must be attributed. While the choice and position of news and feature material throughout the paper undoubtedly reflects someone's opinion, only on the editorial pages may opinion be expressed directly. Readers look to these pages for informed arguments to guide them in making up their own minds about important issues. The best editorial pages offer a broad spectrum of viewpoints, soundly substantiated, and an interesting variety of subject matter and writing styles. The ability to assess these opinions and the fairness with which they are presented is a skill every informed citizen should cultivate.

Whose opinions are they, anyway? First and foremost, they are the opinions of the newspaper: its publisher (owner) and ranking editorial staff members, whose main reason for being in the newspaper business is to influence the course of public life, and perhaps (they may hope) even of history, by presenting the truth as they see it.* Editorials themselves may be written by the publisher, the editor-in-chief, or staff members hired specifically as editorial writers. Some newspapers require junior editors and reporters to write editorials as well, which can be awkard for a reporter assigned to cover the same material in an objective news story. Most editorials are not signed because they are regarded as the opinion of the paper, the "we" of the "editorial we." Some papers, however, believe in individual expression as opposed to corporate expression, and their editorials carry the name or initials of the writer.

There is more to the editorial page and the one opposite it (known as the "op-ed" page) than editorials, however. Here are some of the many ways opinion may be expressed on the editorial pages.

Editorials

Regular columns by established writers
- Nationally syndicated
- Local

Guest editorials, written by people not on the newspaper's staff

Letters to the editor

Editorial cartoons
- Nationally syndicated
- Local

*For a more sophisticated view, you may want to look into a book such as Ben Bagdikian's *The Media Monopoly* (Boston: Beacon Press, 1983) which details how fifty major corporations control what America sees, hears, and reads.

Items of civic or historical interest
Poetry and other miscellaneous items by local writers or staff members
Photography offering:
- Commentary
- Aesthetic value

ACTIVITIES

1. Have students turn to the editorial pages of the daily paper and find as many of the types of expression previously outlined as possible. This could be a scavenger hunt or a simple five-minute "get-acquainted" session.

2. Using the pile of papers that has accumulated during the newspaper study, plan a scavenger hunt that requires finding as complete a list as possible of the preceding items.

The expression of editorial opinion has several purposes, among them to arouse public spirit, to educate, and even to give readers a chance to take issue with the paper. A lively debate on the editorial pages might help to resolve a serious issue; it will most certainly sell more newspapers. Editorials themselves may be on any subject in the world, but more often than not, they have a direct link to an event or issue of current interest. This is known as a "news peg."

II. ANALYZING THE EDITORIALS

ACTIVITY

3. Have students keep a list of all the subjects covered on the editorial pages of their daily paper for a week. Make a chart recording how many times the same subject is treated, and in how many ways—i.e., editorials, columns, letters, cartoons? How many items do **not** have a news peg?

There are four general categories into which editorials usually fall: criticism, praise, interpretation or analysis, and entertainment.

ACTIVITIES

4. Ask students to find an example of an editorial in each of the preceding categories and to write a sentence or two explaining why they placed it there.

5. Ask students to find an editorial with a news peg on the front page of the same paper. Do the facts in the news story support the argument of the editorial writer? This activity can be the basis of class discussion or individual written assignments. See also Chapter 1, ACTIVITY 23.

6. Ask students to keep a week-long check on two or more newspapers, noting how many editorials in each publication had news pegs. What comparisons can be made? What conclusions drawn? See also Chapter 1, ACTIVITY 20.

Editorials, brief and timely as many of them are, provide students with an excellent opportunity to analyze and evaluate expository writing. Activities for this purpose on two levels follow.*

ACTIVITIES

7. For a given editorial, have students answer the following questions:

   - Does it get the point across clearly? How?

   - Does it give explanation, information, direction on an issue? Where?

   - Does it stimulate thinking or motivate action? In what way?

   - Does it appeal to the emotions or to reason? By what means? Sentiment? Satire? (See ACTIVITY 15, page 66.) Straightforwardness?

8. For a closer look at an editorial's structure, try the following:

   - What is the subject of the editorial? Where do you first find it?

   - What position does the writer take in regard to this subject?

   - Does he repeat his opinion? Where? What effect does this have?

   - What arguments does he present to support his opinion? List them specifically.

   - Does he offer any arguments for the opposite side of the question? If so, list them.

   - Where did he get the information for his arguments? Research? Interviewing? Personal observation? Out of the blue? Present evidence to support the inferences you make in answering this question.

III. WRITING EDITORIALS

In the end, the key to understanding is doing. Students should now be ready to try their hand at editorial writing. Some guidelines for writing editorials are listed on reproducible page 64.

---

*Cross Reference: Chapter 9, "English": III. Writing, A. Composition

IV. GUIDELINES FOR WRITING EDITORIALS

1. Choose a topic that is current and interesting to readers.

2. **Try to hang it on a news peg.**

3. Do your homework. You can't make a convincing argument without facts to support it. Document your statements by citing sources.

4. Grab your reader with your opening statement. Some of the same approaches used for news and feature leads work equally well for editorials.

5. Be brief. Long-winded editorials put off readers. But be sure to include the vital points.

6. Present both sides.

7. Use specific examples, analogies, comparison, contrast to give the reader a clear picture.

8. If you criticize, make constructive suggestions. If you praise, don't undermine your credibility by going overboard.

One well-known bit of advice to student editorial writers is: "Tell them what you're going to say; say it; tell them what you've said." A simplistic rule for making sure you have a beginning, a middle, and an end, but it works and is frequently used.

ACTIVITIES

9. Have students find an example of an editorial that follows the preceding pattern and then indicate how it does. It will help them to see basic essay structure.

10. Have students decide on a topic for an editorial and discuss the ways it might be handled. (See ACTIVITY 4, page 62.) Each student should then choose the approach he or she thinks is most effective and write an editorial, sticking to his or her choice. These may be examined and discussed by the class when completed.

11. Have students choose individual topics for editorials and write them. Post the most successful.

V. COLUMNS

Nationally known columnists are quoted, damned, and interviewed by the media. Because syndicates sell the same material to many newspapers, even small papers can provide their readers with the opinions and expertise of highly paid writers and, thereby, with a broader understanding of world affairs. A well-balanced editorial page includes columnists with different political outlooks.*

ACTIVITIES

12. Have students examine the daily paper, or preferably several different papers, for a week and list the columns that appear. Analyze the list for variety of subjects, approaches, and points of view (as in ACTIVITIES 6 and 7, page 63). Which paper do students think is better balanced? Why?

13. Compare syndicated columns with those that originate locally for level of reader involvement, quality of writing, and other values students might suggest. Ask them why it is important to have both types of columns on the editorial pages.

14. Have students compare an editorial and a column on the same subject. Ask them to suggest reasons for any major differences they may discover.

VI. CARTOONS

Many people turn to the editorial page chiefly to enjoy the cartoon, which is almost always political or sociological and almost always satirical. Satire is one of the most difficult literary concepts for students to grasp. While this is not the place for a lengthy treatment of the subject, examining political cartoons can help further their understanding.

*Cross Reference: Chapter 11, "Social Studies": Individual columnists in different subject areas.

ACTIVITIES

15. Provide students with copies of several editorial cartoons and have the class discuss the following:

    – What topic is the "issue" of each cartoon?

    – How does the cartoonist present the topic—literally or metaphorically?

    – If literally, identify the participants. What devices does the cartoonist use to make sure you don't mistake these identities?

    – If metaphorically, what do the various elements in the cartoon symbolize?[1]

    – How does the cartoonist feel about the subject?

    – What is the most obvious device the cartoonist uses to get the point across? (*Answer:* exaggeration, stereotyping)[2]

    – Identify the cartoonist and the origin of the cartoon; either local (rare) or the name of the syndicate.

16. Have each student collect four or five editorial cartoons, mount them, and write a brief analysis of each, based on the items in ACTIVITY 15. These may be posted on the bulletin board.[3]

17. Use a cartoon to illustrate the basic principle of satire:[4] ridicule, either bitter or gentle, of human folly or vice, with the purpose of bringing about reform or at least shedding a sharper light on the situation. Exaggeration, especially through caricature, and humor are the chief devices of cartoon satire. Not to be confused with sarcasm, which is plain cruelty, satire is both cruel and kind: it gives hurt, but only in the interest of society. Irony, another valuable tool of the cartoonist, is neither cruel nor kind. Verbal irony is the discrepancy between what is said and what is meant. Dramatic irony is the discrepancy between what the speaker says or believes and what the reader or audience knows to be true. Irony of situation is the discrepancy between what is expected or ought to be and what actually is true.[5]

18. Let students try their hand at editorial cartoons focusing on a school, local or national issue. Display the results for class enjoyment and discussion.

19. Not only cartoonists, but also editorial writers and columnists employ satire to inform, reform, and entertain. Ask students to find other examples of satire on the editorial pages. You may wish to extend the assignment to discover whether a particular writer is known for satire or whether he or she only uses it occasionally. Discuss how satire may be effective when a direct approach is not.

---

[1]**Cross Reference:** Chapter 9, "English": II. Language, B. Figurative Language

[2]*Ibid.*, I. Reading, B. Literature

[3]**Cross Reference:** Chapter 10, "The Arts": II. Visual Arts, A. Graphics and Design

[4]**Cross Reference:** Chapter 9, "English": I. Reading, *loc. cit.*

[5]*Ibid.*

VII. LETTERS TO THE EDITOR

Unless they contribute to the school newspaper, students aren't likely to be writing editorials or columns for publication. Their opinions, along with those of everyone from their own parents to high-ranking public officials, **can** appear in print, though, as letters to the editor. These are often printed under such headings as "The Voice of the People," or "Reader Response." Letters to the editor may parallel editorials in offering criticism and praise; they may register complaints or defend the position of the writer in some controversy; they may attempt to explain something the writer feels is misunderstood; they may even entertain, sometimes unwittingly.

ACTIVITIES

20. Have students find two letters to the editor, one they consider effective and one they consider ineffective. These may be analyzed in class discussion or as individual written assignments.

21. Have students write letters to the editor in response to an editorial in the local paper, either agreeing or disagreeing with it. Discuss the letters in class, and have students decide which one(s) to send to the paper for publication.

22. Encourage students to write letters to the editor on topics they want to speak out on. If any are published, they should be brought to class.

Letters to the editor must be signed, so the paper can determine if the signer actually wrote the letter. If a paper should print a letter written by someone other than the person who signed it, the paper could be sued. Some papers will withhold the name of the writer on request. Others will not, maintaining that anyone who wishes to express an opinion in print should be willing to stand behind it.

VIII. CHAPTER EVALUATION

Many written activities in this chapter provide opportunity for evaluation. A test on terms and concepts follows on a separate page for convenience in photocopying.

Name _____ Date _____

_____ QUIZ: EDITORIALS _____

I. In the blank before each item in column A, write the letter of the description in column B that best fits it.

A	B
___ 1. Corporate expression	a. Link between an editorial and a current event
___ 2. Publisher	b. Page opposite the editorial page
___ 3. Editorializing	c. The editorial "we"
___ 4. Op-ed	d. Ridicule with the purpose of bringing about reform
___ 5. Column	e. Expressing opinion in factual reporting
___ 6. News peg	f. To cite sources of information
___ 7. To document	g. Gap between what is true and what appears to be
___ 8. Satire	h. Cruel words, intended to wound
___ 9. Irony	i. Owner of the newspaper
___ 10. Sarcasm	j. Regular feature in which a recognized writer expresses his or her opinion

II. Fill in the blanks. (You can continue on the back if you need more space.)

1. The major function of the editorial page is to _____ .

2. Editorials are usually written by _____ .

3. Editorials are not usually signed because _____
_____ .

4. Three things besides editorials that can usually be found on the editorial pages are _____ , _____ , and
_____ .

5. The four main types of editorials are _____ ,
_____ , _____ , and
_____ .

(continued)

Name _____ Date _____

QUIZ: EDITORIALS
(continued)

6. Three purposes of editorials are _____ ,
   _____ , and _____ .

7. What three things are you likely to find in an editorial page cartoon?
   _____ , _____ ,
   and _____ .

8. Newspapers encourage readers to write letters to the editor because
   _____
   _____
   _____ .

9. Letters to the editor must be signed because _____
   _____
   _____ .

10. A good editorial section should have the following characteristics:
    _____
    _____
    _____
    _____
    _____
    _____

© 1985 J. Weston Walch, Publisher

ANSWERS TO
QUIZ: EDITORIALS

I.

1. c	6. a
2. i	7. f
3. e	8. d
4. b	9. g
5. j	10. h

II.

1. Express opinion

2. Publisher, editor-in-chief, editorial writers

3. They are supposed to express corporate (the newspaper's) opinion.

4. Letters, columns, cartoons, poetry, photography, items of civic or historical interest

5. Criticism, praise, interpretation or analysis, entertainment

6. To arouse public spirit, educate, give readers a chance to take issue with the paper (other reasonable ideas acceptable)

7. Caricature, exaggeration, politics, satire (other reasonable answers acceptable)

8. A lively controversy interests readers, helps to sell more papers.

9. The newspaper needs to check authorship to avoid being sued.

10. A broad spectrum of viewpoints—local and national, soundly substantiated—and an interesting variety of subject matter and writing styles

IX. SPACE FOR YOUR IDEAS

Sports, Comics, and Other Special Features

CONTENTS

Sports, Comics, and Other Special Features

After a quick glance at the front page, most of us turn to our favorite page or section of the newspaper. Sports, comics, and entertainment pages give us pleasure. Others, such as weather, the financial pages, classified advertising, and even the obituaries provide us with useful information. Sunday papers have larger sections devoted to these subjects, expanded by a wealth of feature material. In addition, Sunday papers include features not usually found in the daily paper: automotive, travel, the arts, home and garden, and special supplements for seasonal events. Scavenger hunts in the EVALUATION section of Chapter 1, and another at the end of this chapter, are designed to acquaint students with the diversity of subjects at their fingertips in the daily paper. Specific areas of interest will be treated under the appropriate subject in Part II of this book. For example, see Chapter 11, "Social Studies: Economics," for activities that focus on the financial pages, or Chapter 12, "Science: Weather," for ways to utilize the daily meteorological report. Advertising is the subject of Chapter 6. In Chapter 5, we will deal not only with two perennial favorites, sports and comics, but also that essential ingredient of the modern newspaper, photography, plus a word or two about community social and cultural news (including births, deaths, and marriages).

I. THE SPORTS PAGES

The sports pages compete easily with the front page for action and violence. In the matter of lively language, they're way ahead. Sports writing is more informal than news writing, has a vocabulary that is thoroughly understood only by true fans, and has its own version of the rules about editorializing. Sports page stories are basically of two types: the straight news or "who won what" story, and the "viewpoint" story, which includes interpretation and analysis. Often, however, the two approaches are combined, making the sports pages the most freewheeling pages in the newspaper. Some of our most skillful users of the English language have been sports writers, among them Damon Runyon, Ring Lardner, Bob Considine, Heywood Broun, and Walter "Red" Smith.*

The usual components of the sports page are:

> Follow-up story (who won what):
> - straight news, inverted pyramid style
> - viewpoint
> - combination of the above

---

*Cross Reference: Chapter 9, "English": I. Reading, B. Literature; III. Writing, A. Composition

Advance story (before an upcoming event):
- – straight news
- – background
- – prediction
- – combination of two or all of the above

Other features not strictly related to a single contest:
- – news interviews
- – personality profiles
- – historical background
- – human interest

Columns

Scoreboard

Photos

ACTIVITY

1. Have students turn to the sports pages and find examples of as many of the preceding components as possible. Discuss the components of at least one of each type to be certain they see the differences.

II. SPORTS LANGUAGE

Action is the name of the game on the sports page. Vivid headlines and exciting stories are to be expected. Fresh, original use of language is the lifeblood of all good writing, but unintelligible sports jargon and hackneyed phrases like "bingle," "scintillating play," or "vanquished" (when the winner led by one point) are to be avoided. The specialized vocabulary of sports, like that of any trade or profession—the sea, carpentry, medicine, journalism, for example—is essential to describing the tools and equipment, the process and play, the craftsmen and players involved. While the term "jargon" is sometimes used to describe such vocabularies, it is used here in the less favorable sense of "pretentious, unnecessarily obscure," even the "secret" language of an "inside" group. A writer may use jargon to create a character through dialogue, for example, but should avoid "speaking" in that kind of voice himself. The distinction between specialized vocabulary and jargon is not always clear. That may be troublesome to the purist, but should not bother anyone who is intrigued by the evolution and vigor of the living language.* The exercises that follow might also be useful to physical education teachers and coaches.

ACTIVITIES

2. Provide students with copies of a fairly long and reasonably vivid sports story. Ask them to underline all the words that are essential sports vocabulary and circle all the words that are jargon. There will be some arguments in the discussion that follows

---

*Cross Reference: Chapter 9, "English": II. Language, A. Semantics

including good cases for some of the jargon words, a good opportunity to make points about how the language grows and develops.[1]

3. Have students explain the meaning of all underlined or circled words in ACTIVITY 2 above. As a small research project, ask them to discover outside class the meanings of any they can't explain.

4. Ask students to find the description of an elaborate play in a sports story and explain it to the class.[2]

5. Look at the headlines on the sports page. Mark all the verbs and put them into two lists: (A) those used literally and (B) those used metaphorically. (See reproducible page 78, EXAMPLE: VERBS IN SPORTS HEADLINES.)

   - Put a check beside all those that are used more than once.

   - Circle all those you consider hackneyed or overused; note jargon.

   - Underline all those that seem overexaggerated (hyperbolic).[3]

   - Put a star beside any you consider especially vivid or well-chosen.

   - Beside list B, write the "plain English translation" of each verb. What do you think of the changes? Would they improve the page or weaken it? What are some of the reasons the headline writers chose the words they did? (See also Chapter 2, ACTIVITY 14. For a similar exercise, using text of story, see Chapter 3, ACTIVITY 6.)

III. SPORTS WRITING

ACTIVITIES

6. Examine a typical follow-up story of an important sports event and answer the following questions.

   - Who won what and how?

   - What was the sport being played? How can you tell? Could the writer do this on the front page? (Frequently the name of the sport is not mentioned. Only the score or name of some position or the names of the teams identify it—to those who are in the know.)

   - How important was the outcome? A championship, a league standing?

---

[1] See BIBLIOGRAPHY.

[2] **Cross Reference:** Chapter 9, "English": IV. Oral English, A. Speech

[3] *Ibid.*, II. Language, B. Figurative Language

EXAMPLE: VERBS IN SPORTS HEADLINES

This is a sample of a list you might draw up for ACTIVITY 5, marked according to the directions for that activity.

A	**B**
loses	✓(scores) — wins
(is) getting along	nets — acquires
(are) surviving	✓(tips) — beats (*jargon*)
is costly	down — beat
(are) in search of	lands — acquires
tie	(upsets) — beats
look ahead	blank — hold scoreless (*jargon*)
wins	ease past — beat by small margin
skate	<u>hammers</u> — beats fiercely
lead ✓	captures — beats
(is) warned	★ humbles — beats a front runner
stands	✓ post — record a score
drop	(edge) — beat by a small margin (*jargon*)
earn	(is) handed — receives
choose	<u>stuns</u> — beats by a big margin
★ <u>batters</u>	<u>shocks</u> — beats by a big margin
credits	(sparks) — initiates, starts (*jargon*)
	handle — beat easily (*jargon*)
	★ chomp — beat fiercely
	★ prowl past (Panthers) — beat
	✓ trips up — beats
	✓(paces) — (a player) leads team in scoring (*jargon*)

- What spectacular plays are described?

- Who were individual stars?

- What were the weaknesses and strengths of each team?

- How did these affect the outcome?

- Did weather conditions play a part?

- How big was the crowd? What was its mood?

7. Look at the preceding story or another one for the following points.

- Does the writer editorialize or stick to straight reporting?

- Opinion is acceptable in sports writing provided, as in all good editorial writing, the opinion is supported by facts. Does the writer support opinion with facts?

- If this is a straight news story, with no opinion, how does it differ from a straight news story on the front page?

The advance sports story is more complex. It may be straight news, written in the inverted pyramid style, with a news lead. It may be a background story, filling in the history, traditions, or personal lives of the chief participants—really a feature hung on a news peg. Or it may be a prediction story. The last is the most demanding. Predictions must be based on logical analysis of the facts, records, observations, interviews with the coach and players, and most of all, the solid experience of the writer. It must not reflect personal bias or wishful thinking. Of course, it is opinion, or more properly, inference: a statement about the unknown, based on the known.[1]

ACTIVITY

8. Have students find advance sports stories and analyze them according to the above description. Have individual students present examples of each type, rating the story for interest, use of language (based on ACTIVITY 2, page 76), lack of bias and sound support of any inferences or judgments (expressions of approval or disapproval).[2]

IV. SPORTS OPINION

The columns of bylined writers, local and national, are the most legitimate expressions of individual opinion on the sports page as elsewhere. Most are not so blatantly opinionated or colorful as the comments of the controversial TV sportscaster Howard Cosell, for example, but many will stick their necks out, generating a rousing response in the letters on the

---

[1] **Cross Reference:** Chapter 9, "English": II. Language, A. Semantics
[2] *Ibid.*

editorial page. Even those who observe carefully and comment fairly are little safer than the average referee from the jeers and catcalls of ardent fans. The majority of sports writers may try hard to be unbiased, but fans have no such journalistic compunctions.

ACTIVITIES

9. Have students select a "viewpoint" story or column from the sports page and examine it for factual material. They may be able to compare it with a related news story or their own observation, at a local game or one on television. Have them decide whether it is fair or biased, citing specific examples in the story.

10. Have students use the same story or another "viewpoint" story and write a short straight news story in inverted pyramid style, using the facts available.

V. SCOREBOARD

The scoreboard, found on most sports pages, contains all the latest scores, local, state, and national, as well as a variety of other information. Scoreboard format varies with the publication. Some are simple, others exhaustive. Sports-minded students usually master the skill of interpreting them on their own, but everyone should know how to find the basics.

ACTIVITIES

11. Using the scoreboard in the daily paper, conduct a discussion that will prepare students for the following written exercise. (You may have to rewrite this to fit information available in your paper.)

    – What was the score of (your school's) most recent game with (opponent)? Who were the officials?

    – How many points did (player) score?

    – In which college (name of sport in season) game was the highest number of points scored? (Combine both teams' scores.)*

    – Which team in your school's class leads the state (or region) in the current season's championship race? With how many wins and losses?

    – In national sports, how many points did (name of league, team) score in the first period, against whom? Who won? What was the score?

    – Which player from which school leads the state (or region) girls' (basketball, field hockey, soccer, etc.) in scoring?

    – How many sports contests are taking place all over the country *today* according to scoreboard listings?

*Cross Reference: Chapter 13, "Math"

– What game(s) could you watch at 7:30 this evening on which TV channels?

– Who was named to what Olympic team recently?

– What coach, player, or manager has just been signed or named to what major league team?

12. Ask a student familiar with the more involved aspects of the scoreboard to explain one of them ("Heal Points," for example). Use the chalkboard. This is a good exercise in oral exposition.[1]

VI. WRITING YOUR OWN SPORTS STORY

ACTIVITIES

13. Have students bring in copies of sports periodicals such as *Sporting News* (for factual and statistical material) and *Sports Illustrated* and *Sport* magazine (for personality profiles and vivid discussions of all sports), as well as magazines devoted to individual sports. Involve the class in an informal discussion, comparing these magazines with newspaper sports coverage. What does each have to offer that the others do not?

14. Assign the reading of a short story or article by one of the famous sports writers listed at the beginning of this section. In the discussion that follows, lead students to some observations about ways in which the nature of sports themselves may have helped to create the author's style.[2]

15. Have students write a three- to five-paragraph **viewpoint** story, either advance or follow-up, making use of what they have learned in this section.

VII. COMICS

Are comics necessary? Should they do more than amuse? What famous newspapers have no comics?[3] Comics have an interesting history that grew out of fierce competition for readers in the late nineteenth century and was aided by rapid strides in printing technology. The early humorous single-panel cartoons that laughed at the ups and downs of the common man developed side by side with the powerful political cartoons. Both had enormous influence on newspaper sales, particularly in view of widespread illiteracy and the influx of

---

[1] **Cross Reference:** Chapter 9, "English": IV. Oral English, A. Speech

[2] *Ibid.*, I. Reading, B. Literature

[3] The *New York Times*, the *Wall Street Journal*, and the *Christian Science Monitor* are three examples.

thousands of non-English-speaking immigrants. By the 1920s the continuing story strip was developed, and by the '30s, action-packed adventure was introduced. Social commentary, particularly the misfortunes of the little guy, has been part of the comics since the beginning, but by the 1950s more subtle political satire appeared. "Pogo" is an example. Even more sophisticated and controversial is "Doonesbury," which lampoons national politics, so much so that some editors print it on the editorial instead of the comics page. It is still, however, the family sit-com and the plight of the underdog that have the broadest appeal. "Blondie," born in 1930, has been consistently first in reader preference surveys for years, and "Beetle Bailey" is a long-time front-runner. Comics, like political cartoons and columns, have the power to draw readers no matter how bad or dull the "hard" news is.

VIII. DISCOVERING THE COMICS

People who read the comics regularly may be surprised to discover how many details of these pages they have overlooked. The following just-for-fun quiz will test students' observational skills and help them discover a new dimension in the "funnies." (See pages 94–96 in the EVALUATION section at the end of the chapter for lists of questions in ACTIVITIES 16, 17, and 18 that can be photocopied.)

ACTIVITIES

16. Without opening the paper, distribute the following list of TRUE-FALSE questions. FGive students a few minutes to check off their answers, then let them turn to the comics page to see how they have done. Follow with a brief discussion, asking for examples to back up their answers. Or make the whole ACTIVITY oral. Answers may be found on page 89 in the EVALUATION section at the end of the chapter.

   1. All comic strips are meant to be funny.

   2. Comic strips can show action.

   3. Comic strips are silent.[1]

   4. Comic strip characters never grow old.

   5. Comic strips are always divided into frames of equal size.

   6. Comic strip characters don't look like real people.

   7. Comic strips are seldom about the real world. (This could lead to the concept of allegory.)[2]

   8. What comic strip characters say is always in balloons.

   9. Comic strips can improve your vocabulary.

   10. All comic strips tell a self-contained story.

---

[1]**Cross Reference:** Chapter 9, "English": II. Language, B. Figurative Language

[2]See also BIBLIOGRAPHY: Bruno Bettleheim, *The Uses of Enchantment* (New York: Alfred A. Knopf, 1976).

11. Cartoons on the comic pages are not all in strip form.

12. Comic strips use "camera angles," just as movies and television do.

17. On the daily comics page ask students to find, wherever possible:

   - The name(s) of the author/artist of each comic strip.

   - The name of the syndicate that supplies the strip and the copyright date. Very few papers have their own comic strip artists.

   - The date when the strip is supposed to be published.

   - Three symbols other than words[1] that show action (clouds of dust to indicate speed, stars to indicate heavy blows, light bulbs to show ideas dawning in characters' minds, ZZZZ for sleep) and tell what these symbols mean

   - Three unfamiliar words. First figure out what they mean from the context and then look them up to be sure you are right.[2]

   - A comic strip that has no frames.

   - A comic strip in which a narrator, rather than the characters, tells part of the story.

   - A comic strip that doesn't use balloons for characters' words.

   - How thoughts, rather than speech, are indicated.

   (See page 95 for reproducible page.)

18. (For a more advanced level) Have students find examples of the following in the comics and answer any questions that accompany items.[3]

   - A comic strip that isn't funny. Why is it on the comics page?

   - An adventure comic strip.

   - A fantasy world or allegorical comic strip.

   - A romantic comic strip. (Some might call it soap opera.)

   - A science-fiction comic strip.

   - A sit-com comic strip.

   - A comic strip that sees the world from a child's viewpoint. Is it really a child's point of view?

   - A political opinion. Is it satirical? Does it take itself seriously, preach, or simply amuse?

   - A philosophical observation. Is it an old saw or a fresh insight?

---

[1]**Cross Reference:** Chapter 9, "English": II. Language, B. Figurative Language
[2]*Ibid.*, III. Writing, C. Vocabulary
[3]*Ibid.*, I. Reading, B. Literature

- A comic strip that draws attention to a human problem. Is it humorous or serious? Which is more effective?

- An educational comic strip (history, environment, science, for example). Do you learn something new from it? Is it useful or merely superficial? Is it true? How do you find out?

(See page 96 for reproducible page.)

19. Comic strips use stereotypes[1] regularly. Discuss this with students, and have them find examples.

IX. DOING YOUR OWN COMICS

ACTIVITIES

20. Have students name their favorite and least favorite comic strip or character and explain one choice or the other in a brief essay.

21. To reinforce skills learned in earlier chapters, have students write and illustrate a news story based on events in a comic strip.[2]

22. Have students develop their own comic strips, suggesting that they think about some of the things they have learned in the above activities that will make their theme clear.[3] When finished, mount them in an attractive display for the class and visitors to enjoy.

X. COMIC STRIP HISTORY

As they accumulate a history, the comics have developed an increasing fascination for fans, collectors, and even scholars. Here are a few suggestions for extra projects that a few energetic students might pursue, either as written reports or oral presentations.[4]

ACTIVITIES

23. Comics that have become movies, stage shows, or TV programs. Examples: "Li'l Abner," "Peanuts" ("You're a Good Man, Charlie Brown"), "Little Orphan Annie" ("Annie"), "Superman," "Blondie," *et al.*

---

[1]**Cross Reference:** Chapter 9, "English": II. Language, A. Semantics
[2]**Cross Reference:** Chapter 10, "The Arts": II. Visual Arts, A. Graphics and Design
[3]*Ibid.*
[4]See BIBLIOGRAPHY for sources.

24. A genealogy of a comic strip family that has grown up, married, and had children.

25. Comics their parents or grandparents knew.

26. A brief history of comics, illustrated with photocopies, or presented with an opaque projector.

27. A brief history of one genre of comics, such as science fiction.

28. Any original investigation of the world of comics.

XI. PHOTOJOURNALISM

Pictures—"shots" to the photographer, "cuts" to the layout department—are essential to the modern newspaper. Only the *Wall Street Journal* can maintain an inflexible position of never putting a picture on the front page, or anywhere else in the paper. Some tabloids, on the other hand, consist of little else. Every page is plastered with pictures, augmented by very sketchy reporting. The same news values apply to photography as to stories: timeliness, proximity, consequence, prominence, conflict, drama, sex, unusualness, and emotion, captured by the camera lens rather than by the reporter's words. The technology of photography is beyond the scope of this book, but it takes no expert to recognize that a shot of the president of the local bank presenting a check to the United Way is not going to win the National Press Photography award of the year. In fact, some papers have rules about printing such pictures, along with other restrictions, like no more than three people in a group photo and no "mug" shots (a straight-on head-and-shoulders portrait). Others use mug shots to identify columnists and speakers in short interviews, for example.

XII. WHAT MAKES A GOOD NEWS PHOTO?

Action and drama, enhanced by strong contrast and clear but uncluttered details, make good newspaper photos. On the other side of the coin, the ethics of photojournalism require that the photographer respect the privacy and feelings of ordinary citizens in tragic situations (a consideration that is not always honored and that doesn't apply to people in public life). News photos should be honest reporting and not be posed, though pictures accompanying certain types of feature articles have to be set up. Among the most serious considerations in newspaper photography are bias and editorializing. The camera sees everything, sometimes in very damaging or overglamorizing ways. A newspaper photographer usually works with a motor-driven shutter, which works just like a movie camera or an automatic rifle. As long as the button is held down, the film advances automatically, shooting frame after frame. In the darkroom, the photographer may find all kinds of unexpected shots, some of which would certainly slant the viewer's understanding of the situation. These could be either accidental or intentional. A photographer is trained to experiment with camera angles and light to create visual impressions that will move the spectator. Just like a good reporter, however, the photographer must present as objective a report of an event as possible. The final decision about which shots to use is the editor's. Slanting by the use of photography is one of the most controversial areas of criticism in journalism, especially in TV journalism.

Serious slanting could lead to a suit for libel, which is discussed in Chapter 8, "The Newspaper Today," III. Libel. These are a few of the basic criteria for judging the quality of a newspaper's photography:

ACTIVITIES

29. Ask students to clip newspaper photos representing the news values outlined at the beginning of Chapter 2 and label them.

30. Have students go through the daily paper and circle photos that they think violate any of the rules just outlined, and ask them to explain why.

31. Have students collect examples of outstanding news photos and be able to explain why they chose them.

32. Assign a student to find out which photographers won National Press Awards and, if possible, find examples of the winning photos.

33. Using the collection of newspapers gathered for ACTIVITY 16, Chapter 1, assign different papers to individual students and have them rate the photography according to the standards described earlier.

34. A picture is worth a thousand words. Clip and mount newspaper photos, removing cutlines. (See Chapter 1, ACTIVITY 10, item 10, page 7.) Have students write cutlines of not more than 100 words (and remembering the 5 Ws) to describe the pictures. Tell them to use their imaginations and make up names, unless the event and the identities are known to them.

XIII. COMMUNITY, SOCIAL, AND CULTURAL NEWS

Even more than for sports and comics, perhaps, people buy the local paper for news of their friends and neighbors. In the egalitarian eighties, the Women's Pages have been replaced by Family Living sections, and the Society Pages have become Recent Weddings and Engagements. Briefer than in former times and often with the couple pictured (rather than just the engaged girl or bride), these still are an important part of the newspaper for many readers. So are the birth announcements, which have also changed to a degree old-fashioned readers might consider scandalous. Meetings of clubs and organizations, cultural events,[1] and church notes are usually listed in convenient calendar form, as are school lunches and recreation schedules, all part of the community service expected of a local newspaper. Some, especially in rural areas, continue to print "personals"—who had out-of-town visitors on Sunday—a practice scorned by worldly journalists, but sorely missed by some readers when it is discontinued.[2]

---

[1]**Cross Reference:** Chapter 10, "The Arts"

[2]**Cross Reference:** Chapter 9, "English": III. Writing, A. Composition (story/essay starters)

ACTIVITY

35. Locate copies of your local newspaper (ask the paper for help) of ten, twenty, thirty years ago. Have students compare a wedding story, an engagement announcement, the birth announcements, reports of club meetings, etc., for evidence of how language and social customs have changed.* What types of social coverage have been dropped altogether? Note also the obituaries. Have they changed as much? At all?

XIV. OBITUARIES

However a paper might deal with local society and culture (and some of them give short shrift indeed), death is another matter. One of the ironies of journalism is that a reporter, whose goal in life is to work in the thick of fast-breaking live action, invariably gets his or her start writing about the dead. Obituaries are the first assignment of 99 out of 100 cub reporters. It is good training ground. Facts have to be gotten straight, verified with certainty, and written up clearly and simply. Obituaries perform a valuable service. Readers are reminded of social obligations they may want to meet, such as offering condolences, attending the funeral, and sending flowers or memorial contributions. For the bereaved, the painful task of informing the community is taken care of. For the deceased, the obituary is a brief biography which may be the only public memorial of his or her accomplishments on earth. The obituaries of prominent persons are written up well ahead, sometimes years in advance of their deaths, sometimes by themselves. Kept in the newspaper's files (this may be why they are called "the morgue"), these are updated from time to time and ready to run in the next issue after the unhappy event, avoiding the need for time-consuming research.

ACTIVITY

36. Have students study the obituaries in the daily paper, then choose a character from fiction—or the comic strips—and write a short, accurate obituary in standard style.

XV. CHAPTER EVALUATION

In addition to the many opportunities for writing in this chapter, an objective test and a short-answer test follow. For the Scavenger Hunt (page 88), make appropriate substitutions in items 2, 6, 9, and 11, and name a specific film for item 5. In the Short Answer Test (page 92), you can select several questions for a short quiz, or use all for a full-period test.

*Cross Reference: Chapter 11, "Social Studies": IV. Sociology; Chapter 9, "English"; II. Language, A. Semantics

Name _____ Date _____

SCAVENGER HUNT

DIRECTIONS: *Using today's paper, find the following facts as quickly as you can. The index on page 1 could speed you along.*

1. The name and birthplace of the oldest person who died in the last few days.

2. The opponent and the score in your school's latest basketball game.

3. How someone born today should conduct his or her affairs.

4. The clue for 1-Across in the crossword puzzle.

5. At what cinema can you see _____ .
   Who is starring, and what are the show times?

6. What did Charlie Brown say to Lucy?

7. What was the Dow Jones closing average?

8. What time did the sun rise this morning?

9. Where can you get a job as a diesel mechanic?

10. On what channels can you watch the "Today" show? Not just the one *you* watch, but all of them. Include their call letters.

11. What ingredients do you need for a Lucious Lemon Pie?

12. What live concert or play could you see in your area tonight?

ANSWERS TO ACTIVITY 16,
pages 82–83

1. F

2. T (Puffs of dust, lines = speed; stars = heavy blow; facial expressions, skillful drawing = action of all kinds.)

3. F (Words like "thud," "pow," "crash," etc., and assorted symbols = sounds.)

4. F (Many examples of comic strip characters who grow up are available.)

5. F

6. F (Many are animals or caricatures, but many others, though romanticized, are representational.)

7. F (Both soap opera type comics and human comedy types are supposedly about the real world. Animal and fairy tale comics are often allegories of the real world. Fantasies like "Superman" and science fiction may not be.)

8. F

9. T (See ACTIVITY 17, item 5, page 83.)

10. F (Many of the stories go on for years; others have episodes that last a few days to a few weeks.)

11. T (Many comics pages include one or more single-frame cartoons. These may also be scattered throughout the paper.)

12. T (Closeups, mid-distance views and long shots, and varied lighting effects frequently employed, especially by the more "realistic" artists.)

Name _____   Date _____

_____ **OBJECTIVE QUIZ: TERMS** _____

In the blank before each item in Column A, write the letter of the description in Column B that best fits it.

A	**B**
____ 1. Obituary	a. Exaggeration
____ 2. Damon Runyon	b. Obscure language used by insiders, not understood by most people
____ 3. "Viewpoint"	c. Several frames, showing an episode in comics
____ 4. Scoreboard	d. Written material that explains a picture
____ 5. Jargon	e. Bordered section of a comic strip
____ 6. Literal	f. Prophecy of how an event will turn out
____ 7. Hackneyed	g. Story that expresses opinion
____ 8. Hyperbole	h. Picture
____ 9. Advance	i. Image or sign that stands for an idea
____ 10. Prediction	j. Clipping file
____ 11. Inference	k. Table of sports statistics
____ 12. Judgment	l. Generalized image of a group or class of people
____ 13. Follow-up	m. Beginning reporter
____ 14. Frame	n. Right to print
____ 15. Pow!	o. Famous sports writer
____ 16. Strip	p. Actual meaning (of words)
____ 17. Copyright	q. Statement about the unknown, based on the known
____ 18. Symbol	r. Head and shoulders portrait
____ 19. Balloon	s. Overused
____ 20. Stereotype	t. Story about an upcoming event
____ 21. Cut	u. Statement of approval or disapproval
____ 22. Mug shot	v. Brief biography of a person who has just died
____ 23. Cutline	w. Standard sound of heavy blow in comics
____ 24. Cub	x. Rounded border containing conversation in comics
____ 25. Morgue	y. Story about the outcome of an event

ANSWERS TO
OBJECTIVE QUIZ: TERMS

1. v	10. f	19. x
2. o	11. q	20. l
3. g	12. u	21. h
4. k	13. y	22. r
5. b	14. e	23. d
6. p	15. w	24. m
7. s	16. c	25. j
8. a	17. n	
9. t	18. i	

Name _____ Date _____

_____ SHORT ANSWER TEST _____

Answer each question in one to five complete sentences.

1. What are the major differences between sports writing and news writing?

2. What rules should a sports columnist observe when making predictions about a game or season?

3. Why do you think writers of sports stories and headlines invent so many new words? What pitfalls must they avoid when doing this? What are some of the positive results?

4. Give three reasons why comics help to sell newspapers.

5. Identify and explain briefly two ways in which comics are valuable and two ways in which they could be harmful.

6. What are some of the requirements of a good newspaper photograph?

7. What services does an obituary perform?

8. Why is obituary writing good training for a cub reporter?

ANSWERS TO
—————— SHORT ANSWER TEST ——————

1. Sports writing is more vivid and informal. It has a special vocabulary and is editorialized more freely than standard news writing.

2. A sports columnist should base predictions on facts, logical analysis, observation, statements of coaches and players, and personal experience. He or she should not be influenced by personal bias or wishful thinking.

3. Sports writers need to describe the same kinds of events over and over without being boring. They also need to fit headlines into limited space. They have to avoid both hackneyed language and jargon that no one can understand. The advantages are that many learn to use language very skillfully and vigorously. Some even become famous writers, like Damon Runyon or Heywood Broun.

4. Everyone needs a break from the serious business of the world. People get caught up in the stories or learn to love the characters. People are also lazy and like to get the story without having to read a lot of words. They like comics that reinforce their own ideas. People who can't read very well, or can't read English, can enjoy the comics.

5. Comics can help improve your vocabulary. They often use difficult words, which are easier to understand because of the pictures. They give you a laugh after a rough day. They can offer insights on life and politics that may be educational. On the negative side, they can make people lazy readers. They encourage superficial thinking and thoughtless generalizations about people, as in stereotypes. They can present inaccurate information about the real world of facts and human relations.

6. A good newspaper photo should have action, drama, interesting contrast, clear details. It should be uncluttered—no more than three people in a group shot—and not be cliché—the same old thing. It should be honest reporting and have the same news values as news stories. An ethical photographer should consider the feelings and privacy of ordinary people caught up in tragedy. Although people in public life are usually fair game, even here the photographer and editor must be careful to avoid bias or editorializing by showing them at an unfair disadvantage or overglamorizing them through choice of shots or camera angles. Another rule that sometimes has to be broken is that pictures shouldn't be posed. Posed pictures can be necessary for certain kinds of feature articles.

7. Obituaries tell people's friends and neighbors about a death in the family so they can send flowers, go to the funeral, and offer sympathy. They save the bereaved from having to spread the news, and they memorialize the dead person.

8. Obituaries require accurate reporting, careful checking of information, and clear, simple writing—the most important skills a beginning reporter can learn.

Name _____ Date _____

ACTIVITY 16
_____ TRUE OR FALSE QUESTIONS _____

T   F

____ ____ 1. All comic strips are meant to be funny.

____ ____ 2. Comic strips can show action.

____ ____ 3. Comic strips are silent.

____ ____ 4. Comic strip characters never grow old.

____ ____ 5. Comic strips are always divided into frames of equal size.

____ ____ 6. Comic strip characters don't look like real people.

____ ____ 7. Comic strips are seldom about the real world.

____ ____ 8. What comic strip characters say is always in balloons.

____ ____ 9. Comic strips can improve your vocabulary.

____ ____ 10. All comic strips tell a self-contained story.

____ ____ 11. Cartoons on the comics pages are not all in strip form.

____ ____ 12. Comic strips use "camera angles" just as movies and television do.

Name _____ Date _____

ACTIVITY 17
——————— COMIC STRIP SEARCH ITEMS—1 ———————

On the daily comics page, find the following wherever possible.

1. The name(s) of the author/artist of each comic strip.

2. The name of the syndicate that supplies the strip and the copyright date.

3. The date when the strip is supposed to be published.

4. Three symbols other than words that show action.

5. Three unfamiliar words. First figure out what they mean from the context, and then look them up to be sure you are right.

6. A comic strip that has no frames.

7. A comic strip in which a narrator, rather than the characters, tells part of the story.

8. A comic strip that doesn't use balloons for the characters' words.

9. How thoughts, rather than speech, are indicated.

Name _____ Date _____

ACTIVITY 18
_____ COMIC STRIP SEARCH ITEMS—2 _____

In your newspaper comics, find the following.

1. A comic strip that isn't funny. Why is it on the comics page?

2. An adventure comic strip.

3. A fantasy world or allegorical comic strip.

4. A romantic comic strip. What other way could you describe it?

5. A science fiction comic strip.

6. A sit-com comic strip.

7. A comic strip that sees the world from a child's viewpoint. Is it really a child's viewpoint?

8. A political opinion. Is it satirical? Does it take itself seriously? Preach? Or is it simply amusing?

9. A philosophical observation. Is it an old saw or a fresh insight?

10. A comic strip that draws attention to a human problem. Is it humorous or serious? Which is more effective?

11. An educational comic strip. (History, environment, science, for example.) Do you learn something new from it? Is it useful or merely superficial? Is it true? How do you find out?

XVI. SPACE FOR YOUR IDEAS

Advertising:
More Than Half the Paper

CONTENTS

Advertising: More Than Half the Paper

I. WHY ADS?

Cynics have been known to comment that the news in the paper is just there to hold the ads together, and sometimes, at busy merchandising seasons like Christmas, Easter, and back-to-school time, it almost seems that way. Actually, to stay economically healthy, newspapers try to maintain an average of 60 percent advertising to 40 percent editorial material. The amount of space sold to advertisers governs the number of pages in the newspaper on any given day. If not enough ads are sold, the editors have to cut back on the number of stories printed. If more ads than usual are sold, the proportion of ad space can go as high as 75 percent.

II. FUNCTIONS OF ADVERTISING

It is advertising sales that pay the costs of printing and newsgathering and the salaries of production and editorial staffs, as well as make the profits the owners expect. A financially successful newspaper can afford the top-notch reporters and equipment that make it possible to offer the public a quality production.

Advertising has two other important functions. It serves businesses, by informing the public of what they have to offer, and it serves readers by letting them know what goods and services are available. By creating a demand for products, advertising stimulates business and can thereby help to create more jobs. The amount of money spent for newspaper advertising in any given year exceeds the combined total spent for radio and television. This is because of newspapers' tremendous mass penetration into the homes of every community. It is also because the price of newspaper advertising is within the reach of many more small businesses than radio and television prices. A newspaper's ability to attract advertisers depends on its **circulation**, the number of copies it sells every day through subscriptions and individual sales. Circulation is so important to advertisers that most newspapers belong to the Audit Bureau of Circulation (ABC), which verifies this number. Circulation figures are usually included on a newspaper's advertising **rate card**, which lists the prices for advertising space. A rate card can be obtained from any newspaper's advertising department.

III. TYPES OF ADVERTISING

There are three types of newspaper advertising:

General advertising: advertisements by national companies designed to inform readers about new products, to convince them of a product's superiority, and to keep the product's name before the public. Magazine and television advertising is general advertising. While these media have the advantage of color, action, and slickness, general ads in newspapers can be tailored to target directly the needs and tastes of consumers in a given geographical area.[1]

Retail advertising: advertising by local merchants and service companies. Retail ads are an important service to readers, providing information about prices, sales, and availability of the things they need and want. Retail advertising is also known as "display" advertising, because it often involves graphic arts design and illustrations.[2]

Classified advertising: class-ads, as they are called, are the marketplace for private individuals and small businesses. They might even be called the poor person's stock exchange, for here people of limited means can both make a little needed cash by selling unwanted possessions and find used items economically. Classified ads are usually inexpensive and are known to get results. Through them a person can buy or sell anything from a home to a hamster.

ACTIVITIES

1. Have students find examples of general, retail, and classified ads and list differences among them. Some possibilities:

   - General ads may employ a greater variety of persuasive techniques,[3] whereas retail ads stress bargains, specials.

   - General ads do not usually include specific prices, while retail ads do. You might call general ads "features" and retail ads "spot news."

   - Classified ads use many abbreviations. Their language is more likely to be original than slick.

2. Have students make three lists of persuasive words:[4]

   - Those found in general ads.

   - Those found in retail ads.

   - Those found in classified ads.

   Ask them to account for any differences they may find. *Clue:* General ads are prepared by Madison Avenue-type agencies; retail ads may be prepared by local advertising agencies (which can be just as sophisticated) or by the business people themselves; classified ads are written by you and me, often with the help of the person taking them down at the newspaper office. Ask students to identify the chief differences between ad writing and news writing. (*Answer:* Slanting is the name of the game in ad writing, taboo in news writing.)

---

[1] **Cross Reference:** Chapter 9, "English": II. Language, A. Semantics
[2] **Cross Reference:** Chapter 10, "The Arts": II. Visual Arts, A. Graphics and Design
[3] **Cross Reference:** Chapter 9, *ibid.*
[4] *Ibid.*

3. Have students create a display ad to sell a product.[1]

4. Have students make a list of the categories under which advertisements are placed in the classified section. Lead them to see why they are called "classified" ads.

5. Have students spend twenty to thirty minutes reading the classified ads and collecting the following:

   - Three items that look like good buys.

   - Two jobs they might apply for.

   - A house they would like to live in.

   - Information they didn't know was available, such as legal notices, personals, courses, wanted to buy, etc.

   - The most fascinating ad of any kind that they run across.

IV. WRITING YOUR OWN ADS

ACTIVITIES

6. Have students clip the instructions for preparing a classified ad and any specials the paper offers, such as "four lines for four days for four dollars." Have each student prepare an ad for a ten-speed bicycle, with the intention of appealing to the buyer. They should make sure to follow rules carefully and take advantage of any specials. Afterwards, compare the results, having the class decide which versions are the most effective.[2]

7. Following the plan of ACTIVITY 6, have students write an ad for something they want to sell. If they actually place the ad, ask them to report the results to the class.[3]

8. Have students study the "Positions Wanted" ads and write an ad designed to get them a job.[4]

9. Have students clip and mount a real estate ad, then write a description of the property, keeping an eye open for hidden meaning, such as "handyman's dream," "partly finished," etc., or a ridiculously low price. Or use a used car ad. This could be fun.

---

[1]**Cross Reference:** Chapter 10, "The Arts": II. Visual Arts, A. Graphics and Design

[2]**Cross Reference:** Chapter 14, "Consumer Education"

[3]*Ibid.*

[4]**Cross Reference:** Chapter 15, "Career Education"

10. Have students create their own display advertisements.*

A student design entered in the "Design an Ad" competition and published in the *Times Record*, Brunswick, Maine (along with stories, illustrations, and editorials contributed by students in area schools in celebration of Newspaper in Education Week). *(Reprinted by permission of Yankee Pedalers, Inc., Brunswick, Maine.)*

***Cross Reference:** Chapter 10, "The Arts": II. Visual Arts, A. Graphics and Design

11. Have students take one column from any part of the classified ads and list the abbreviations they find, then write the meaning of each abbreviation. Compare the results with those of the class or of a partner. For any that can't be deciphered, assign a student to check with the newspaper's classified ad desk.

12. Using the daily paper, have students plan a shopping trip in which they purchase or pay for the following:

    – A needed article of clothing

    – A wanted recreational item (sports equipment, records, etc.)

    – Lunch

    – Something to be repaired, from a shoe to a car

    – Ingredients for dinner at home

    – An after-dinner movie

    They must clip the ads that determine their choices and add up the cost. This could be an individual project, but it would be much more fun to do in groups. Have the class review the results and decide which group is getting the most for its money. Not only price, but also quality must be considered.*

V. CHAPTER EVALUATION

Students' understanding of advertising can be gauged by their participation in the preceding activities. For an extra check, a simple objective test follows.

---

*Cross Reference: Chapter 14, "Consumer Education"; Chapter 13, "Math"

Name _____ Date _____

_____ **QUIZ: ADVERTISING** _____

Fill in the blanks.

1. The average rate of ads to news in a paper is _____ percent ads to _____ percent news.

2. Ad sales pay for the cost of _____ and _____ .

3. Ads serve businesses by _____ .

4. Ads serve readers by _____ .

5. Ads can create jobs by _____ .

6. More money is spent on newspaper advertising than on radio and television because _____ _____ .

7. General advertising is _____ .

8. Retail advertising is _____ .

9. Classified advertising is _____ .

10. The chief difference between ad writing and news writing is _____ _____ _____ .

ANSWERS TO
———————— QUIZ: ADVERTISING ————————

1. 60 percent ads, 40 percent news
2. newsgathering and printing (or production)
3. telling the public what they have to offer
4. letting them know what is available, at what prices
5. stimulating business
6. newspapers reach into more homes with information about what is available locally, and newspaper ads cost much less
7. advertising by big national companies
8. advertising by local merchants and service businesses
9. advertising by private individuals and small businesses
10. ad writing is supposed to slant the reader's opinion and persuade, and news writing is supposed to be unslanted

VI. SPACE FOR YOUR IDEAS

CHAPTER 7

News and History

CONTENTS

News and History

I. REPORTING HISTORY AS NEWS

This chapter takes a somewhat different approach than those preceding.* The history of the newspaper can be fascinating, but not if it's just a chronological catalog of dry facts. The summary that follows may be reproduced and given to the students in booklet form, using the special title page that precedes it as a cover. Or the summary can be used to prepare lecture notes on the history of newspapers. In either case, the summary has been written with a special project in mind. The idea is to assign selected activities to students, who will be asked to use newsgathering, writing, editing, and production knowledge gained through activities in preceding chapters to produce a short history of the newspaper in the form of a two- to four-page tabloid. Some will research and write "news" and feature stories on given topics. Others will be editors, headline writers, illustrators, layout, and pasteup people. It would be lovely if this tabloid could be reproduced, so that each class member has a copy (11″ x 17″ photocopies are available in many places). The pages can, however, be posted on the bulletin board so that each class member can study them individually while others have a quiet work period. A quiz can then be tailored to the students' own reporting of the history of the newspaper.

Students will be more inclined to do "reports" if they have a strict format of three to five short paragraphs in inverted pyramid news style or feature style. Both types appear in the assignments. Their classmates will be much more inclined to pay attention when they can read each other's work in published form. There will be opportunity for comment on the quality of coverage. For example, does it include the basic Five Ws? These gentle reminders, along with journalistic discipline, will reinforce skills in finding and organizing material. Reading, editing, and headline writing as the information takes concrete form will make remembering the basic history of the newspaper much easier. At the same time, newspaper structure and style will be given one more round of reinforcement. The fun of hands-on creation is also an important factor. Don't be alarmed at the number of references in the text that follows. The essential highlights of the history of newspapers will be starred in the ACTIVITIES list, although you should feel free to make your own selection according to the area you wish to emphasize, the grade level, and the time available. Of course, you can use the following outline for whatever other purpose you wish. A basic objective test covering the material is included at the end of the chapter.

---

*Cross Reference: Chapter 11, "Social Studies": Since this entire chapter is of interest to all branches of social studies, no further cross references will be made, except to other chapters.

NEWS AND HISTORY
REPRODUCIBLE
BOOKLET

NEWS AND HISTORY

FROM THE DAWN OF TIME

Humankind's insatiable **desire** to know what's happening is as old as the race. Even older is the **need** to know, for survival—a need we share with our animal relatives, one no less urgent today than it was two million years ago. An antelope or an Australian aborigine sniffing the morning breeze receives news as vital to him as the news we receive in the morning paper may be to us. The **right** to know is a much more recent and more controversial development. Whether to satisfy desire, need, or right, news is a commodity essential to existence.

From the age of stone tools to the age of stone castles, bards and messengers carried news of heroic exploits and natural disasters from campfire to campfire and from court to court. In the Middle Ages, annual fairs brought whole country-sides together as much for the exchange of news and gossip as for the exchange of goods. Even before that time, the Romans had what could be considered the first newspaper, a hand-copied news sheet called *Acta Diurna* (*Daily Acts*) that was posted about the city as early as 59 B.C. But it wasn't until the invention of moveable type by Johann Gutenberg in the fifteenth century that the early rudiments of the modern newspaper, with its implications for the course of history, made their first appearance. As Marshall McLuhan pointed out, print made possible the private contemplation of other people's ideas, the creation of individualistic patterns of enterprise and monopoly, and the wide dissemination of radical new thought. "The hotting up of the medium of writing to repeatable print intensity led to nationalism and the religious wars of the sixteenth century."*

Among the earliest newspaper prototypes were accounts of a war in Dalmatia authorized by the Magistracy of Venice in 1566, to be read and posted in public places. To obtain a copy, a citizen paid a small gold coin called a *gazetta*, the origin of "gazette" as the name for a small news sheet. What is thought to be the oldest true newspaper in Europe was the 1609 *Aviso* published in North Germany (in what city scholars aren't sure). By 1620, newspapers were being printed in many German cities and had spread to Belgium and Holland. The first newspaper in London appeared in 1621; the first in Paris, in 1631. The oldest continuously published newspaper first came out in the Swedish court in 1645 and is still in existence.

---

*Marshall McLuhan, *Understanding Media: The Extensions of Man* (McGraw-Hill Book Company: New York, 1964), page 37.

THE PRESS AND THE STRUGGLE
FOR FREEDOM

As the printing process made literary material cheaper and more available, the desire for literacy and hence for some kind of public education developed. The standardization of spelling and the uniformity of print helped to focus ideas more clearly than oral accounts; government policies and their effect on events could be observed; the possibility of questioning authority arose. Thus began the struggle for freedom of the press, which is the very heartbeat of democracy.

When William Caxton set up England's first press in 1476, it was with the blessing of King Edward IV, who encouraged Caxton's intention to bring continental culture to the country in the form of classical literature. The first English newspaper was still two centuries away, but books that were published in the interim sometimes contained ideas that were disturbing to the status quo. With the consolidation of royal power under the Tudors, the press fell under the monarch's watchful eye. Henry VIII published a list of prohibited books in 1529, and in 1534 the Crown issued a proclamation requiring printers to have royal permission to operate. The press was controlled by the Privy Council, which began making arrests for the printing of politically oriented street ballads in 1540. As might be expected, an underground press quickly developed, peddling broadsheets that angered the king. During several centuries of repression, nursery rhymes like "Humpty Dumpty" and "Hector Protector" served as political cartoons in disguise, and many a traditional folksong has a revolutionary background. The Stationers Company, established by Queen Mary in 1557, ordered weekly searches of London printing houses. The infamous Star Chamber arrested and hanged William Carter in 1584 for printing pamphlets favoring the Catholics. And so it went.

Despite the penalties, printers continued to defy the government. "Corantos," news sheets describing the events of the Thirty Years' War on the continent, began appearing in the 1620s, often criticizing the foreign policies of James I, a criticism for which the editors paid dearly. The first paper to report domestic news was John Thomas's *Diurnall Occurences*, in 1644.

Under the leadership of rebellious Puritans in the Long Parliament, the Star Chamber was abolished in 1641. Poet John Milton's famous essay, "Areopagitica," one of history's most eloquent pleas for freedom of the press, was published in 1644. Using arguments that have been echoed by many an editor and public speaker in the ensuing three centuries, Milton declared:

> ...though all the winds of doctrine were let loose to play upon the earth, so truth be in the field, we do injuriously by licensing and prohibiting to misdoubt her strength. Let her and falsehood grapple; who ever knew truth put to the worse, in a free and open encounter.

Though Milton's words had little effect on events of his day, they were picked up a century later by revolutionary leaders everywhere, particularly in America. But sad to say, after the execution of Charles I, Milton himself became a government censor for the Commonwealth under Oliver Cromwell. With the restoration of Charles II in 1660, printing was again limited by royal authority, though not so severely as in Tudor times. One Benjamin Harris, an adventurous London journalist, tangled with the Crown once too often and in 1686 was forced to flee to America, where he became the country's first newspaper publisher.

The licensing act eventually expired in 1694, not because of any new enlightenment, but for political expediency. The eighteenth century saw the birth of the first English daily, the *Daily Courant*, in 1702. Under Samuel Buckley, it became the first real **news**paper. Buckley insisted on factual reporting, rather than gossip, and presented both sides of political issues. At the same time, the famous essayists Richard Steele and Joseph Addison were publishing the *Tatler* and the *Spectator*, and Daniel Defoe was editing *Mist's Journal*. Thomas Gordon and Robert Trenchard produced the "Cato Letters," published in the *London Journal* and the *British Journal* between 1720 and 1723. Dealing with liberty, representative government, and freedom of expression, the Cato Letters were in great demand in both England and America. Jonathan Swift, as editor of the *Examiner*, satirized the political power struggles of the early 1700s. Later in the century, Samuel Johnson was influential in removing the ban forbidding the reporting of activities in the House of Commons. Throughout the eighteenth century, the Crown enacted a series of stamp taxes which had the desired effect of raising the price of newspapers out of the reach of the common people. The Stamp Act of 1765 is usually regarded as one of the causes of the American Revolution, although it was just as unpopular in England as in the colonies. Stamp taxes continued in Britain into the 1850s, restricting the growth of the newspaper industry there. Despite temporary setbacks, freedom of speech and the press continued to gain ground as the monarchy retrenched. As one author observed, the more secure a government is, the less it fears criticism by the press. "The progress of press freedom shows that the press belongs to those who rule. . . . If power is concentrated in the hands of a monarch or an elite group, there is no need for the public to receive information or ideas pertaining to political or social matters. . . . On the other hand, if the public participates in government, it must have access to information in direct ratio to its place in the political scheme."*

THE BIRTH OF AMERICAN JOURNALISM

Meanwhile, on the other side of the Atlantic, the first colonists were too busy conquering the wilderness to worry about civilized amenities like newspapers until about 1700. World news was supplied by English papers, and individual colonies were too widely separated to exchange American news. Benjamin Harris, mentioned above, actually published the first American newspaper. *Publick Occurrences, Both Foreign and Domestick*, made its single appearance on September 25, 1690, in Boston. Because he spoke out plainly on matters of public policy, Harris got into trouble with Massachusetts (British) authorities, in violation of licensing restrictions. After only one issue, the paper attained the dubious

---

*Edwin Emery, *The Press and America* (Prentice–Hall, Inc.: Englewood Cliffs, NJ, 1972), pp. 15, 16.

distinction of being the very first publication to be banned in Boston. A more innocuous journal, the *Boston Newsletter*, initiated by John Campbell in 1704, continued for 15 years.

The *New England Courant*, founded in 1721 by James Franklin, Benjamin's elder brother, was the first American newspaper actually to oppose the party in power, as well as the first to launch an editorial crusade by presenting news in a dramatic form that generated public interest. Along with a serialization of Defoe's *Robinson Crusoe* and reprints from many English journals including the *Spectator*, the *Courant* also ran the anonymous "Silence Dogood Letters," authored by the publisher's young apprentice, Benjamin Franklin.

James Franklin courageously challenged the Massachusetts church authorities and the British government. These activities landed him in jail, but upon his release, he continued his spirited appraisal of authority until he was forbidden to publish by the General Court. To evade the decree, James made Benjamin his publisher. The wily younger brother, released from apprenticeship bond for the purpose, seized the opportunity to make off to Philadelphia, where he soon became the major publisher of the period. He took over management of the *Pennsylvania Gazette* in 1729 at the age of 24 and retired 18 years later as president of a chain of newspapers and a prosperous man, to devote himself to the cause of the American Revolution. Franklin's *Pennsylvania Gazette* is probably early America's most famous newspaper.

Another important journalistic figure in Colonial America was John Peter Zenger, whose trial for "Scandalous, Virulent and Seditious Reflections on the Government" became a landmark in the history of press freedom. For the first time, the truth of the statement in question was recognized as a defense in a libel case.

The annals of the American Revolution include many courageous journalists, none better known than Samuel Adams, who is remembered not only as an untiring reporter, but also as an unscrupulous mudslinger. His efforts were a major factor in the success of the Revolution. Thomas Paine, author of *Common Sense* and the *Crisis Papers*, is equally famous. Other patriot journalists who played significant roles were Benjamin Edes and John Gill of the *Boston Gazette* and Isaiah Thomas of the *Massachusetts Spy*.

THE PRESS IN THE NEW NATION

The cornerstone of press freedom in America was laid with the first article of the Bill of Rights, the first ten amendments to the Constitution.

> Congress shall make no law. . .abridging the freedom of speech or the freedom of the press.

The early years of the new country were marked by violent controversy between conservative and liberal factions, in which the press took a leading role. Matters got so hot that the Alien and Sedition Act of 1798 was passed by Congress and actually did abridge freedom of the press for several years.

As the country grew, so did the newspaper business. The first daily newspaper was the *Pennsylvania Evening Post* in 1783. Others quickly followed both in the big port cities of the east coast and further inland. The press expanded, not only geographically but also sociologically. Gradually, states dropped restrictive voting laws, and "universal" suffrage (for men only) became the rule. The craving for knowledge grew with the country. In a country with few schools and textbooks, newspapers became the chief instrument of education. Between 1810 and 1825, the number of printing businesses tripled. The election of Andrew Jackson in 1824 signaled the era of the "common man." The first labor paper, the short-lived *Journeyman Mechanic's Advocate*, appeared in 1827 along with the *Mechanic's Free Press* (which was more successful). Still to emerge was a general newspaper the common people could afford.

A means of mass producing newspapers was needed. The printing machine of Colonial times was the wooden English common press which, when operated by two journeymen and an apprentice, could produce 200 impressions an hour at best. A much improved hand press was developed in 1822 by Peter Smith of R. Hoe and Company. This was supplanted in 1830 by a steam-operated power press perfected by Hoe. It was finally possible to print a paper that would sell for only one cent, compared with six cents (the price of a good meal in those days) for the commercial papers. The "penny press" would revolutionize American journalism and politics.

The first such paper to succeed was the *New York Sun* ("It Shines for All") which appeared in 1833. It was sensational, vulgar, and entertaining. It was supported by volumes of advertising, another developing aspect of the newspaper industry. It was printed on a new cylinder press at the rate of 1,500 papers per hour. The *New York Herald*, the *Baltimore Sun*, and others soon joined the penny press ranks.

THE AMERICAN PRESS COMES OF AGE

One of America's best-known journalists emerged at this time. In 1841, Horace Greeley founded the *New York Tribune*, a penny paper of considerably more substance than its predecessors. Once papers like the *Sun* had got people reading, their skills improved, and their demands became more sophisticated. The *Tribune's* weekly edition had more readers than any other publication of the period. The time was soon ripe for the next step upward: the *New York Times*, established in 1851 by Henry J. Raymond. The rapid growth of the newspaper in the nineteenth century can be attributed to three major factors: improved printing technology, a burgeoning reading public, and improved communications.

Newsgathering soon took precedence over the exposition of ideas. People would rather read about events than editorial opinions, as the penny press had proved. Rather than print whatever news happened along as in earlier days, the search for news began. The reporter became the key person. The "scoop," getting a fast-breaking story into print ahead of the competition, became every editor's priority and every reporter's dream. As early as 1808, there was a Washington correspondent for a Philadelphia paper. The practice became firmly established in the 1830s. Foreign news traveled faster with the development of the steamship. Carrier pigeons joined the communications system, and the Pony Express could bring news from New Orleans to New York in seven days. The railroad soon entered the picture, and a special locomotive was hired in 1841 to carry President Harrison's inaugural address from Washington to Baltimore, Philadelphia, and New York. Samuel F. B. Morse's invention of the telegraph in 1844 would stand as the greatest leap forward until the telephone appeared in the 1870s.

It wasn't long after the arrival of the telegraph that a group of New York newspapers arranged to receive news in common. In 1848, the first "wire service," the Associated Press, was formed. News arriving by steamship in Halifax or Boston was relayed to New York, and soon Philadelphia and Baltimore papers joined the association.

With news coming in rapidly from all points and an eager public awaiting it, technology was hard pressed to keep up. Richard Hoe's revolving press of 1846 mounted the type for each page on a curved iron form attached to cylinders. One such press, with six cylinders, could print 12,000 impressions an hour. The invention of stereotype plates vastly improved the process. A mold or matrix (later called a mat) took the impression of the type, and a curved mold of the whole page could be made by pouring hot lead into the matrix, a process in use until the development of offset printing in the mid-twentieth century.

As the pioneers moved west, so did newspapers. By the 1850s, they were established in frontier towns and cities from coast to coast.

A HOUSE DIVIDED

The widening cultural and economic chasm between the South and the North that eventually led to the Civil War began much earlier, and the press played an important role in polarizing the issues. In 1831, William Lloyd Garrison, best known of the abolitionists, established his fiery journal, the *Liberator*, in Boston. Another abolitionist editor, Elijah Parish Lovejoy, died defending his press from an angry mob in Alton, Illinois, in 1837. There were also black abolitionist journalists: among them John B. Russwurm, the Reverend Samuel Cornish (who founded *Freedom's Journal* in 1827), and the most celebrated of them all, Frederick Douglass, whose *North Star* began publication in 1847.

At the opposite end of the spectrum were the southern "fire-eaters," deeply devoted to the cause of secession, like Robert Barnwell Rhett, editor of the *Mercury* in Charleston, South Carolina. On less extreme ground stood opponents of slavery like Horace Greeley, who also opposed radical abolitionists; William Cullen Bryant, editor of the *New York Evening Post*, who offered enlightened defense of freedom; and Henry Raymond of the *New York Times*, who was lukewarm to abolitionism, but a staunch supporter of Abraham Lincoln.

During the Civil War, the question of military censorship of the press arose for the first time. Never before had reporting been so aggressive, its techniques so thorough. An interesting phenomenon was the development of what is now known as "AP style." Newspapers of the period adhered to extreme political positions. The Associated Press reported to papers of differing loyalties. Consequently, its dispatches had to stick to straight factual reporting, a practice that has become one of the foundations of modern journalism.

THE PRESS IN THE AGE OF NATIONAL EXPANSION

The press, like every other aspect of American life, picked up the pieces and made a new start after the Civil War. Changes in content and writing style to satisfy new public tastes, the shift away from personal influence toward corporate ownership, and new technology all played their part. Two important developments were the growing emphasis on objective reporting and the increasing independence of editors from political pressures. Among the many famous names in journalism between 1865 and 1900, those of Joseph Pulitzer and William Randolph Hearst[1] stand head and shoulders above the rest. In his statement of policy for the *St. Louis Post-Dispatch,* which he founded in 1878, Pulitzer set the tone for the "new journalism" of the period. He declared that the paper would serve no one but the people, print only the truth, criticize the administration, oppose all fraud, and advocate "principles and ideals rather than prejudices and partisanship."[2] Pulitzer purchased the *New York World* in 1883. The *World* soon broke every publishing record in America, vastly expanding its circulation through the popular appeal of its sensational but accurate reporting and its campaigns in behalf of the common people. Hearst, who launched his career in similar fashion with the *San Francisco Examiner,* arrived in New York in 1895 to purchase the *Journal* and challenge Pulitzer's leadership. They were soon engaged in a "yellow journalism" war.

During the same period, organizational and technological changes that would create the newspaper of the twentieth century were taking place. The modern newspaper staff, with its specialized duties (described in Chapter 1) gradually emerged. Women reporters began to take their place in the newspaper world. The summary lead developed. Cooperative newsgathering agencies, in addition to the newly reorganized Associated Press, were formed. The Atlantic cable, laid in 1866, linked American agencies by telegraph with their counterparts in Europe. Advertising became a national industry. Monthly magazines, some of whose names are still household words, were founded. The linotype machine was invented by Ottmar Mergenthaler in 1886. The automatic folding machine was perfected by 1890. That, together with advances in the papermaking process, made it possible with a web press to print 48,000 12-page newspapers per hour.

[1]Orson Welles's classic film, *Citizen Kane,* was based in part on the saga of William Randolph Hearst.

[2]Quoted by Don C. Seitz, *Joseph Pulitzer: His Life and Letters* (New York: Simon and Schuster, 1924), p. 101.

New type designs, color printing, and engraving processes that made possible the use of photographs all heralded a new era in newspaper graphics. It was not long before the wireless, patented by Guglielmo Marconi in 1901, was used for the first trans-Atlantic radio dispatch from England to New York in 1907. Shortwave was to follow in 1924, further shrinking time and distance, an advance surpassed only when the first satellites brought the entire world into simultaneous television contact in the early 1960s.

THE NEWSPAPER'S HEROIC AGE

The first half of the twentieth century could be called the heroic age of the American newspaper. The empires of Pulitzer, Hearst, and Midwesterner Edward Scripps were forming. Other famous figures were Adolph Ochs of the *New York Times* and William Allen White of the *Emporia* (Kansas) *Gazette*. Crusading against the evils of society gained momentum. The newspapers were joined in these efforts by the "muckraking" magazines of the era, led by *McClure's*, *Collier's*, and *Cosmopolitan*. Among the best remembered muckrakers are Ida Tarbell, who exposed the unfair business practices of Standard Oil and John D. Rockefeller; Lincoln Steffens, who attacked corruption in government; Samuel Hopkins Adams, who uncovered patent medicine fraud; and above all, Upton Sinclair, whose 1906 novel, *The Jungle*, appalled the country with its revelation of the horrors of the Chicago stockyards. The exploits of dozens of famous newspaper figures of the period make fascinating reading. Among them were Peter Finley Dunne, Franklin P. Adams, Cyrus H. K. Curtis, Edward K. Bok, Walter Winchell, Dorothy Kilgallen, David Lawrence, Heywood Broun, Drew Pearson, Walter Lippmann, Dorothy Thompson, Ernie Pyle, Westbrook Pegler, Elmer Davis, Edward R. Murrow, Joseph Alsop, Roscoe Drummond, Harold Ross, Grantland Rice, Alexander Woollcott, and many more.

No sooner had the golden age of the newspaper in America dawned than its doom was foreshadowed by the very magnitude of its endeavors. As standardization became the hallmark of advancing technology and society, the rugged individualism that gave each paper its unique character began to go out of style. Competition gave way to merger, and newspapers joined the ranks of the huge corporations. The number of English-language daily newspapers in the United States reached its all-time peak of 2,600 in 1910. By 1930, the number had declined to 1,942, and by 1970 to 1,748. In 1983 it was 1,708. The usual reasons given for this decrease have been the skyrocketing costs of newspaper operation and the competition for audience from the electronic media. Group ownership and the development of newspaper chains was on the rise, a trend that continues. The Hearst and Scripps-Howard organizations dominated the national scene before 1930. Today the largest is the Gannett Company, owner of 88 dailies from coast to coast. One of the most remarkable newspaper monopolies today is that of the Australian magnate Rupert Murdoch, who operates on an international scale.

Returning to other important developments of the twentieth century, the question of wartime censorship arose again in both world wars and has continued as military emergencies of varying character have become the rule rather than the exception. But censorship of "classified" military information, for which justification can often be made, was not the most serious threat to freedom of speech. The Espionage Act of 1917, purportedly to prevent "disloyal" Americans from aiding the enemy, actually had the (intended) effect of curtailing the civil liberties of anyone who spoke out against wartime government policy. Hardest hit were socialist organizations and German-American publications, but pacifists and isolationists (among them William Randolph Hearst) were also castigated. The Trading-with-the-Enemy Act of 1917 and the Sedition Act of 1918 were even stronger. Responses paralleled Milton's "Areopagitica."

Following World War I, the newspaper industry joined the Jazz Age with the introduction of tabloids, their full-page pictures and screaming headlines more sensational than even the "yellow journalism" of the previous era. The *Daily News*, founded in New York in 1919, was the country's most widely circulated paper by 1924, when Hearst jumped on the bandwagon with the *Daily Mirror* and Bernarr Macfadden, publisher of *Physical Culture* and *True Story* magazines, added the *Daily Graphic*, the most lurid of them all. "Gutter journalism" was the name of the game. The *Daily Graphic* died in 1932, and the *Mirror* closed in 1963. The *Daily News* still flourishes, along with fifty or more tabloid-format papers of widely differing editorial quality.

A more significant contribution to modern journalism was the new interest in interpretive and specialized reporting that took root in the 1930s and 1940s. Many of these columnists and investigative reporters are still writing.

Photojournalism developed apace with other newspaper technology. An important advance was the vast improvement in picture reproduction quality made possible by the offset printing process. The zenith of photojournalism was reached with the large-format *Life* magazine added in 1937 by Henry R. Luce to his already flourishing *Time* magazine empire. *Look* provided competition the following year. The impact of these magazines, which heralded the age of visual, nonverbal mass communication (and according to Marshall McLuhan, the demise of print and the return to the values and perceptions of a pre-literate culture)* was tremendous. Unfortunately for them, the reporting of news through visual images was quickly taken over by the television industry. *Look* lasted until 1971. *Life* experienced a decline in the seventies and retrenched as a slender monthly in 1979. For the art of photography and the standards of photojournalism, they remain a landmark.

More recent episodes in the history of journalism, such as coverage of the Vietnam War, the Watergate scandal, and the news blackout on the Grenada "incident" in 1983, not only involve other media but also bring up important contemporary issues more appropriately dealt with elsewhere.

---

*From the jacket blurb, Marshall McLuhan, *Understanding Media: The Extensions of Man* (McGraw-Hill Book Company: New York, 1964).

II. NEWSPAPER IN HISTORY PROJECT

As stated at the beginning of this chapter, the aim of this project is to have students come up with their own history of the newspaper rather than to read it from a book or listen to a lecture. After a brief introduction to the idea, have students choose editing and production jobs as follows:

- Editors—one per page, who decide which stories go on each page and are responsible for individual pages

- Layout designers/pasteup people—one or two per page

- Headline writers—one or two per page

- Artists and headline printers—one or two per page

A suggested format:

- Front page—major news stories

- Page 2—editorials and some features

- Page 3—features, art work

- Page 4—more news

With tabloid-size newsprint (usually available in the art room), four columns would make a readable layout, typed single space with an elite typewriter. Alternatively, a full-size (or tabloid) newspaper could be produced by using sections of the blackboard as pages, **taping** the stories, headlines and illustrations in place. This would both provide an instant display and make possible the inclusion of more material. Depending on the grade level, it may be necessary for the teacher (or a parent volunteer) to type the stories. See Chapter 2, "What Is News?": V. Headlines, VI. Layout, and ACTIVITY 17 for additional help.

Since these jobs can't be done until the material has been written, the next step is to have the same students select the stories they will write or the graphics they will produce. (Or you may want to assign them.) In order to spread responsibility and avoid classroom bureaucracy, exchange stories at random for student editing, with teacher help and rewrite suggestions. When the stories are in their final form, typed in columns, students can change hats and assume the editorial and production duties.

In order for this project to go smoothly and not take a disproportionate amount of time, check available resources for required information beforehand. You may wish to obtain some materials listed in the BIBLIOGRAPHY through interlibrary loan or other sources if they are not in your school library. Students can begin with information from the booklet, but in many cases, more detail is needed than is furnished here. If they find conflicting information and if the source is reliable, by all means accept it. These should not be exhaustive reports, however, but brief news-style accounts as indicated. The value of this practice in finding salient points and organizing them logically cannot be overestimated.

The suggested activities beginning on page 126 follow the text of the "News and History" booklet. The major emphases are on the development of printing and newsgathering technology, outstanding personalities, and the evolution of freedom of the press. The numbers of certain activities that follow a continuing historical thread have been repeated at several points in the text. Activities marked with an asterisk (*) represent major highlights in newspaper history.

III. ACTIVITIES 1–49

ACTIVITIES

* 1. Draw an illustration depicting a bard telling the news at the court of an ancient chieftain and write a caption of no more than twenty-five words explaining the picture.[1]

 2. Write a one-paragraph facsimile of *Acta Diurna* in Rome for March 15, 44 B.C. (the day Julius Caesar was assassinated).[2]

* 3. *(First in **Technology of Printing** series of student reports)* Write a three-paragraph straight news story about Johann Gutenberg's invention of moveable type.

 4. Write a three-paragraph editorial of interpretation on Marshall McLuhan's theory of hot and cool mediums.[3]

 5. Write a three-paragraph feature about early newspapers in Germany, Sweden, and Italy, including an explanation of the origin of the "gazette."

 6. Write a three-paragraph news story about William Caxton's introducing the printing press in England.

 7. Find a nursery rhyme or folksong that is a political commentary in disguise, and use it as the basis of an editorial cartoon.[4]

* 8. *(First in **Freedom of the Press** series of student reports)* Write a four-paragraph analytical news story on the suppression of the press under the Tudors in the sixteenth century.

 9. Write a one-paragraph filler on "Corantos" *or* on John Thomas's *Diurnall Occurences.*

*10. Design a box containing the famous quote from Milton's "Areopagitica" on freedom of the press and hand-letter it.[5]

 11. Draw a political cartoon drawing attention to Milton's acceptance of the job of government censor in Oliver Cromwell's regime.[6]

*12. Write a four-paragraph front-page news feature on Benjamin Harris, rebel journalist.

---

[1]**Cross Reference:** Chapter 10, "The Arts": II. Visual Arts, A. Graphics and Design
[2]*Ibid.*
[3]**Cross Reference:** Chapter 9, "English": II. Language, A. Semantics
[4]**Cross Reference:** Chapter 10, "The Arts": II. Visual Arts, A. Graphics and Design; "English": I. Reading, B. Literature
[5]**Cross Reference:** Chapter 10, "The Arts": II. Visual Arts, A. Graphics and Design
[6]**Cross Reference:** Chapter 9, "English": I. Reading, B. Literature; III. Writing, A. Composition

13. *(Second in the **Freedom of the Press** series)* Write a four-paragraph review for the "books" column on the major political essayists of the eighteenth century in England *or* write a satirical column of four paragraphs on today's political power struggles using an essay by Jonathan Swift as a model.[1]

*14. Taking the position of his enemies, Cotton and Increase Mather, write a three-paragraph letter to the editor on the exploits of James Franklin *or* write a two-paragraph straight news story on the same subject.

15. Read several of Benjamin Franklin's "Silence Dogood" letters, and write a letter to the editor about a current school or town problem in the same style.[2]

*16. Write a five-paragraph news feature on Benjamin Franklin and the *Pennsylvania Gazette*.

17. *(Third in **Freedom of the Press** series)* Write a three-paragraph editorial on the importance of the trial of John Peter Zenger to the free press in America.

18. Write a four-paragraph profile of Samuel Adams, political agitator.

19. Write a three-paragraph book review summing up and commenting on the importance of a work by Thomas Paine.[3]

20. Write a four-paragraph news feature on the *Boston Gazette* and the *Massachusetts Spy* and on the activities of their publishers.

*21. *(Fourth in the **Freedom of the Press** series)* Write an analytical feature of four or five paragraphs on suppression of freedom of speech and the press by the Alien and Sedition Act of 1798, the Espionage and the Trading-with-the-Enemy Acts of 1917, and the Sedition Act of 1918.

22. *(Second in the **Technology of Printing** series)* Draw a labeled diagram of the English Common Press or another early wooden press used in the Colonies, and include a one-paragraph explanation of its operation.[4]

*23. *(Third—and last—in the **Technology of Printing** series)* Write a five-paragraph feature, outlining the development of printing technology since Colonial times and its implications for the newspaper industry. Include the Hoe steam press of 1830, the revolving press of 1846, the invention of stereotype plates, linotype, automatic folding machine, and the offset printing process.

24. Write a three-paragraph human-interest feature on the "penny press" in the 1830s.

---

[1]**Cross Reference:** Chapter 9, "English": I. Reading, B. Literature; III. Writing, A. Composition
[2]*Ibid.*
[3]*Ibid.*
[4]**Cross Reference:** Chapter 10, "The Arts": II. Visual Arts, A. Graphics and Design

25. Write a three- or four-paragraph biographical profile of Horace Greeley.

*26. Write a science-page feature of four or five paragraphs on the development of communications technology and its effect on the growth of the newspaper industry. Include the inventions of the telegraph, the steamship, the Atlantic cable, the telephone, the wireless, shortwave, and satellites.[†]

*27. Write a news feature on the founding of the Associated Press of New York in the 1880s. Make reference to its prototype, the Associated Press, founded in 1848, and other newsgathering agencies that developed in America and Europe during the latter part of the nineteenth century. Don't go over five paragraphs.

28. Write a four-paragraph human-interest feature on frontier newspapers that went west with the pioneers. Include a well-known frontier journalist like Mark Twain or a colorful paper like the *Tombstone* (Arizona) *Epitaph*.

29. Write a letter to the editor of two or three paragraphs responding (negatively or positively) to an editorial by William Lloyd Garrison.

*30. *(Fifth in the **Freedom of the Press** series)* Write a spot-news front-page story of four paragraphs on the destruction of the press and murder of Elijah Lovejoy in Alton, Illinois.

31. Write a feature story (four paragraphs) on black abolitionist journalists, focusing on Frederick Douglass.

32. Write a four-paragraph editorial of criticism *or* praise about the moderate pro-Lincoln press *or* the secessionist fire-eater press of the Civil War period.

*33. Taking the point of view of *either* a liberal journalist *or* a military expert, write a five-paragraph "syndicated" column relating military censorship in the Civil War, in the First and Second World Wars, and in the Vietnam War.

34. Write a biographical profile of three or four paragraphs on Joseph Pulitzer.

35. Write a biographical profile of three or four paragraphs on William Randolph Hearst.

*36. Write a news feature of three paragraphs on the "yellow journalism war" between Pulitzer and Hearst in New York in the 1890s.

37. Write a five-paragraph feature on famous women reporters of the nineteenth century.

38. Write a feature story about three or four famous magazines of the 1800s and their modern counterparts. Use no more than four paragraphs.

[†]**Cross Reference:** Chapter 12, "Science": IV. Physics

39. Assume the position of a graphic arts expert, and write a four-paragraph analytical article on the "new look" in newspaper printing of the late 1800s and early 1900s.

40. Write a three-paragraph news story on the founding of the Scripps-Howard newspaper chain.

41. Write a three-paragraph obituary for Adolph Ochs of the *New York Times*.

42. Write a four-paragraph biographical profile of William Allen White.

43. Write a letter to the editor expressing concern about the unsavory practices uncovered by the "muckrakers."

44. Read an article by one of the muckrakers, and write a three-paragraph review of it, including a sentence or two of biographical information

*45. Research an outstanding newspaper figure of the past in your own town, city, or region. Write a feature story (five paragraphs) about his or her most important achievement.

*46. Write a four-paragraph analytical article for the financial page on the status of three or four of the biggest modern newspaper chains.[†]

47. Write a three-paragraph spot news story on Rupert Murdoch's most recent acquisition, including a few highlights of his other holdings.

48. Write an editorial of praise or criticism on one or two tabloid newspapers you find on today's newsstands, including a few words about their Jazz Age predecessors.

49. Write a three-paragraph biographical profile of one of *Life* magazine's famous photographers (for example: Margaret Bourke-White, Alfred Eisenstadt, or Robert Capa).

[†]See *The Media Monopoly*, by Ben H. Bagdikian (Beacon Press: Boston, 1983).

Name _____ Date _____

CHAPTER EVALUATION—
_____ OBJECTIVE TEST _____

In the blank before each statement, write the letter of the item below it that best completes the statement.

_____ 1. Before the invention of the printing press

     a. there was no such thing as news.

     b. news was carried by bards and messengers.

     c. people depended on carrier pigeons for long-distance communication.

_____ 2. Johann Gutenberg invented moveable type in

     a. 55 B.C.   b. the 1400s.   c. the 1800s.

_____ 3. An early type of newspaper whose name survives in modern form was the

     a. stereotype.   b. *Aviso.*   c. *gazetta.*

_____ 4. King Edward IV was pleased when William Caxton established a press in England because

     a. he wanted advice on how to rule.

     b. he liked to read.

     c. he wanted to upgrade England's culture.

_____ 5. Henry VIII and other Tudor monarchs

     a. encouraged freedom of speech and press.

     b. made it difficult and dangerous to express controversial opinions.

     c. put a stop to all printing in England for some time.

_____ 6. John Milton wrote a famous defense of freedom of the press called

     a. "Areopagitica."   b. *Common Sense.*   c. *Acta Diurna.*

_____ 7. The first English daily newspaper, the *Daily Courant,* appeared

     a. about 1600.   b. about 1700.   c. about 1800.   d. about 1900.

(continued)

Name _____ Date _____

CHAPTER EVALUATION—
_____ OBJECTIVE TEST _____
(continued)

_____ 8. The first American newspaper, *Publick Occurrences, Both Foreign and Domestick,* which appeared in 1690

    a. was an immediate success.

    b. lasted for 15 years.

    c. was banned after only one issue.

_____ 9. James Franklin's *New England Courant*

    a. challenged both the British governors and the Massachusetts church elders.

    b. was not very popular.

    c. played along with the wishes of the authorities.

_____ 10. After James Franklin stopped printing, his younger brother Benjamin

    a. continued publishing the *New England Courant.*

    b. gave up the newspaper business.

    c. went to Philadelphia and founded the *Pennsylvania Gazette.*

_____ 11. Which of the following was *not* an active journalist for the American Revolution?

    a. Samuel Adams   c. Benjamin Edes

    b. Tom Paine   d. Horace Greeley

_____ 12. The development of newspapers for the common people was *most* dependent on

    a. the election of Andrew Jackson.

    b. the invention of a cheaper way to mass produce newspapers.

    c. the spread of railroads.

_____ 13. The "penny press" was

    a. oriented toward educated readers.

    b. unsuccessful.

    c. vulgar and sensational.   *(continued)*

Name _____ Date _____

CHAPTER EVALUATION—
OBJECTIVE TEST
(continued)

_____ 14. Which of the following did *not* contribute to the rapid growth of the newspaper industry in the nineteenth century?

    a. The invention of the steamship

    b. The invention of the telegraph

    c. The invention of the rotary press

    d. The invention of satellites

_____ 15. William Lloyd Garrison was known for his

    a. fiery editorials demanding the abolition of slavery.

    b. calm, reasoned approach to the slavery issue.

    c. advocacy of seceding from the Union.

_____ 16. The most famous black journalist of the Civil War period was

    a. Booker T. Washington.

    b. Frederick Douglass.

    c. Eubie Blake.

_____ 17. The first association for cooperative newsgathering was founded in

    a. 1776.   b. 1848.   c. 1891.   d. 1922.

_____ 18. Joseph Pulitzer and William Randolph Hearst were

    a. famous frontier journalists.

    b. best known for the prizes they gave out.

    c. contenders for the title of America's foremost newspaper publisher at the turn of the century.

_____ 19. The muckrakers

    a. wrote articles advocating new agricultural practices.

    b. exposed government and corporate fraud.

    c. wrote lurid stories about sex and crime.

(continued)

Name _____ Date _____

CHAPTER EVALUATION—
OBJECTIVE TEST
(continued)

_____ 20. There were more daily newspapers in existence in America in _____ than at any other time.

    a. 1910   b. 1920   c. 1940   d. 1960   e. 1980

_____ 21. Since the ratification of the Bill of Rights in 1791, freedom of the press

    a. has been assured forever.

    b. is frequently threatened by special interests and must be constantly guarded.

    c. has been in jeopardy only during wartime.

_____ 22. Of the tabloid newspapers that made their debut in America along with the Jazz Age, the only survivor is

    a. the *Daily News.*

    b. the *Daily Graphic.*

    c. the *Daily Mirror.*

_____ 23. Which of the following is *not* a reason for the decline in the number of daily newspapers?

    a. The expansion of television

    b. The high cost of newspaper production

    c. The offset printing process

    d. The merging of newspapers into huge corporations

_____ 24. *Look* magazine was *most* outstanding in the 1940s for its

    a. photojournalism.

    b. worldwide reporting.

    c. sensational inside stories.

_____ 25. The largest newspaper chain in America today is

    a. the Hearst Corporation.

    b. the Gannett Company.

    c. the Scripps–Howard organization.

ANSWERS TO
CHAPTER EVALUATION—
_____ OBJECTIVE TEST _____

1. b	10. c	18. c
2. b	11. d	19. b
3. c	12. b	20. a
4. c	13. c	21. b
5. b	14. d	22. a
6. a	15. a	23. c
7. b	16. b	24. a
8. c	17. b	25. b
9. a		

V. SPACE FOR YOUR IDEAS

CHAPTER 8

The Newspaper Today

CONTENTS

The following excerpt has been reprinted by permission of the author, Michael D. Harmon, from the *Portland Press Herald*, Portland, Maine, December 6, 1983.

. . .To me, fairness in any story is an achievable goal. I would define it to include:

✔ A decent respect for the opinions of those with whom the writer disagrees.

✔ An honest attempt to present as many views of the topic at hand as time and space permit, bearing in mind that subsequent stories might be necessary to do a truly adequate job.

✔ Attention to the constant nagging of a proper journalistic conscience which says, "Have I answered—or explained why I can't answer at this time—all the important questions a reader might have about the subject of my story?"

✔ And writers and editors must, when their topic is a controversial one, be fully aware of their own feelings and opinions on the issue and be certain those feelings haven't materially affected the content, display or other treatment of the story.

Please notice this last aspect is a long way from "suppressing" or "denying" those feelings—and a long way especially from not having them at all.

Would you want stories written about vital issues by persons who were so dead of soul that they were not, too, aroused by them? Such moral and intellectual eunuchs exist, I'm sure, but few of them become journalists.

When journalists are more honest about their own positions to ourselves, our readers will come to trust us more. And we'll be printing, if not "objective," at least fundamentally honest and fair stories. . . .

The Newspaper Today

The newspaper in the age of technology is a vastly different animal from the newspaper of a hundred, or fifty, or even ten years ago. Electronics not only have revolutionized news-gathering and printing techniques but also have given birth to its competition. At the same time, with the world of journalism now embracing radio and television as well as print, the age-old battle for freedom of the press and speech has spread to all three fronts. This chapter examines briefly the differing uses and values of electronic and print media and touches on some highlights in the continuing dialogue concerning journalistic rights and responsibilities.

I. HAVE RADIO AND TELEVISION MADE NEWSPAPERS OBSOLETE?

Class discussion and student surveys conducted in Chapter 1 undoubtedly revealed the degree to which radio and television have replaced the newspaper as the major information sources for many people. Yet the very technological advances that have made them possible have also resulted in a deluge of printed matter. More books, magazines, and newspapers are being printed and read than ever before. While the number of daily newspapers themselves in the United States has never regained the 1910 peak, circulation—the number of individual copies of newspapers printed and sold—has increased steadily. The newspaper as an institution is by no means dying, for several important reasons. Newspapers carry **detailed news of local interest and a wealth of other information** that no national or even local broadcast medium could devote the time to. You can **select** what you want to read by glancing at the headlines rather than sitting in front of the set waiting for something interesting. You can read your selection far **faster** than a broadcaster could read it aloud. Furthermore, the information is **permanent**. It doesn't get away. (Try taking down a recipe from a Julia Child show.) The **economic factor** clinches the continuing existence of newspapers, which are the major advertising medium for thousands of local and regional businesses, large and small.[1] Newspapers are big business, engaged in serious competition for their share of the gross national product. They are the fifth largest manufacturing business in the country, in terms of employment.[2] The following ACTIVITIES will help students discover for themselves the relationship between television, the radio, and the newspaper in their lives.

---

[1]**Cross Reference:** Chapter 6, "Advertising: More Than Half the Paper"
[2]**Cross Reference:** Chapter 11, "Social Studies": V. Economics

ACTIVITIES

1. Before beginning the fact-finding ACTIVITIES below, conduct an oral poll and discussion on personal preferences. Have student pollsters at the board record:

   - A show of hands indicating which one of the three (TV, radio, newspaper) each would choose if they could have only one.

   - What they like about TV

   - What they don't like about TV

   - What they like about radio

   - What they don't like about radio

   - What they like about newspapers

   - What they don't like about newspapers

2. List on the board the major TV channels (network, public, and cable) and major radio stations in your area. Ask for a show of hands indicating who watches or listens to each. If most listen to only a few, take care to assign students to neglected areas. Be sure to include Public TV, both news and the "MacNeil-Lehrer News Hour," Public Radio's "All Things Considered," and the 24-hour cable TV news, as well as any special news programs scheduled for that evening. The following day, have students work in groups according to the channels/stations they have covered. Each group first goes through the daily paper and checks off every story, editorial, or picture with explanatory caption that was covered on broadcasts. Next have them **count** all the items of information that were not on the broadcast. One representative for each channel or station then records on the board the number of stories it covered and the number in the paper that it did not. Now, have the entire class join in a brief discussion comparing their findings.

3. Follow up ACTIVITY 2 by returning to the groups and analyzing the **types** of stories that did not make the broadcast news. What stories were left out that they considered important, and what stories were broadcast that they thought unimportant? Reasons for broadcast choices should be suggested and discussed by the entire class.

4. Choose two or three major stories that will certainly be on the upcoming evening broadcast news. Again, make sure all important sources are covered. Have students take note both of time allotted to each and to details included in the broadcasts. The next day, working in groups again, have them compare the broadcast coverage with the print coverage. See what conclusions they can draw.

Some of the differences between broadcast and print news coverage they may discover are:

   - When you watch/hear broadcast, if you don't catch it, you can't go back and read it over. (This is exploited by advertisers, who catch people with emotional appeals, knowing they can't check back on what [if anything] was said. Some put their entire advertising budget into broadcast rather than print for this reason.)

- With radio you have to picture what's happening.

- Print you can re-read or go back to later when you have time. You also have a permanent and detailed record to clip and save, or to go back and look up later in library files.

- Newspapers have more details about everything.

- Newspapers have local stories and a wider variety of regional stories than do broadcasts.

- Newspapers can cover local news more easily, because reporters with pencils, tape recorders, and cameras are more mobile than TV camera people.

- Ads in newspapers help you find local services and compare prices. Some are on local radio, but very few on TV.

- People who work with computers and video screens all day may prefer to relax with a newspaper instead of adding to their "video fatigue."

- Newspapers provide much more in the way of opinion, analysis, and in-depth features on specialized subjects.

ACTIVITY

5. Assign a five- to seven-paragraph analytical feature or a three- to four-paragraph editorial discussing the differences between broadcast and print news coverage discovered during the previous ACTIVITIES.

To return to the advances of technology, radio news has been with us since the 1930s; television, since the 1950s; and the movie newsreels, which preceded television in the visual news field, date back to World War I. Films, videotapes, and recordings demonstrating the often fascinating differences between pioneer non-print media and today's slicker fare are available.[1] The future has even more possibilities in store. Cable television now caters to as many special interest groups as print does. The "electronic newspaper" is already in the experimental stage. In response to the increasing difficulty of delivering newspapers on time, caused by traffic congestion in the streets and mail congestion in the post office, technology is being developed that will store newspaper pages in computer banks. With the proper hookup, consumers can dial an index and select information to be viewed a page at a time on the home TV screen.

ACTIVITY

6. As a special project, interested students might want to investigate some of the electronic newspaper prototypes such as CeeFax, Teletext, and Videotext.

---

[1]See APPENDIX for details.

II. RESPONSIBILITY AND FREEDOM

Despite the many changes that have characterized the evolution of the newspaper, its basic function remains the same: to keep people accurately informed about the world around them, so they can make the intelligent personal and public decisions necessary to living in a free society. When the information reveals threats to life, liberty, health, peace, or the environment, the press[1] is said to be carrying out its "watchdog" function. The Watergate scandal of 1973, in which *Washington Post* reporters Carl Bernstein and Bob Woodward uncovered political improprieties that eventually led to the resignation of President Richard M. Nixon, is one of the most famous "watchdog" operations of recent years. Questioning the activities of kings, presidents, institutions, and vested interests at all levels of society can be a dangerous and exciting game, one in which the press has on more than one occasion indulged in self-serving sensationalism at least, and sometimes in even greater irresponsibility.

III. LIBEL

The right of access to information has to be balanced by the responsibility of reporting fairly and honestly and by the more delicate questions of journalism ethics beyond legal guidelines.[2] Does the public's "right to know" extend to the printing of lurid details that in no way serve serious public interest, merely to satisfy voyeuristic curiosity? Matters of taste cannot be legislated, but libel laws do protect private individuals except when they become involved in areas of public interest. Public figures and officials are protected only if they can prove deliberate lying or extreme recklessness in verifying information on the part of the newspaper.

IV. FAIR TRIAL

The question of reporting courtroom proceedings, particularly in spectacular cases, pits the right of the public to information against the right of the accused to a fair trial. The press currently agrees that some restrictions on reporting are necessary to protect persons on trial from prejudicial "trial by newspaper," so long as such restrictions are mutually agreed upon rather than decreed by the court.

V. RIGHT TO KNOW

The "right of access" or "freedom of information" concerns the "right to know" about the affairs of government, from activities in the Pentagon right down to those of the local board of selectmen. In 1984, a reporter for a Maine newspaper called attention to the importance of the state's Freedom of Access law. Local government committee meetings used to be held privately, and many decisions—such as loan approvals, contract awards, and disposal of tax-acquired property—went to the "right" people, he said. The Freedom of Access law provides that the deliberations of public officials be conducted openly and

---

[1]"The press" today refers also to radio and TV news media, which share this responsibility with newspapers.

[2]The 1982 film, *Absence of Malice*, explores this question dramatically.

that the records of their actions be open to public inspection. "It guarantees everyone—not just the news media, who are given no special privileges—the right to know what their government is doing," he wrote. Most states have laws similar to Maine's.

VI. PROTECTION OF SOURCES

Should a reporter be required to reveal his or her sources of information for stories involving criminal investigations? On the one hand, the point has been made that no citizen, not even the president of the United States, is protected by the First Amendment from telling what he or she knows in court. If you have seen a crime committed, you have to testify. You do not, however, have to report hearsay. From another point of view, reporters can be seen in the same position as lawyers, doctors, priests, and ministers, who are not required to reveal information told them in confidence. The argument is that if a reporter is required to reveal his or her sources of information, the sources will dry up. The purpose of the story, to enlighten the public, will thereby be thwarted. Although many states have "shield laws" that give reporters this privilege, federal courts do not necessarily recognize them. The dilemma will probably never be resolved, because it involves conflicting rights and conflicting interpretations of the Constitution. Each case is settled differently, and reporters still go to jail for standing on their journalistic integrity.

VII. CENSORSHIP

Censorship, whether of "classified" military information or "obscene" material, presents another perennial problem for the free press.[1] Standards vary greatly in different communities, and those of society as a whole have changed dramatically in the last twenty-five years. The commonly applied test for obscenity is "whether to the average person, applying contemporary community standards, the dominant theme of the material taken as a whole appeals to prurient interests."[2] Later decisions added the test of "redeeming social importance."

The press must contend with more subtle restraints as well, such as the "managed news" and the "credibility gap" of the Lyndon Johnson administration, the unconscionable news blackout of Ronald Reagan's 1983 invasion of Grenada, and the ongoing manipulative practice of news "leaks" (to say nothing of the control exercised by corporate owners of newspapers, mentioned below).

VIII. FREEDOM OF THE PRESS SUMMED UP

Edwin Emery sums up the question of freedom of the press succinctly:

> Those who are faithful champions of freedom recognize that arbitrary action against the weak and the obscure, against the nonconformist and the radical, against the foolish and the crafty, usually leads later on to arbitrary action against others. Freedom of the press, save when publication constitutes a legally determined clear and

---

[1]**Cross Reference:** Chapter 7, "News and History": ACTIVITY 33; Chapter 11, "Social Studies": ACTIVITY 40

[2]*Roth* v. *United States*, 354 US 476 (1957)

present danger to society, cannot be denied in one case without jeopardizing the constitutional guarantees of all.

...The great importance of a period of "crisis credibility" (such as the Vietnam War period) is that people learn anew that all freedoms are dependent upon freedom of speech and the press. These are never secure, never certain, always capable of being lost.[1]

Since situations that test one or another of the above aspects of freedom of the press arise regularly, the following ACTIVITY is of a general nature, to be adapted to an issue current at the time of study: a logical application of the basic premise of this book—that the newspaper brings the real world into the classroom.

ACTIVITIES

7. Select a current, or the most recent available, issue involving freedom of the press. Have students collect for study as many news articles, analyses, editorials, cartoons, etc. as they can find on the topic. Divide the class into three groups: the plaintiff and its attorneys, the defendant and its attorneys, and the Supreme Court. Each side must present its argument. If the case has not been settled, the classroom Supreme Court must make a well-considered decision. If the case has already been settled, the classroom judges must take the roles of the Supreme Court justices and explain their positions. If the case is settled soon after the classroom hearing, it will be interesting to compare the decision of the class with that of the U.S. Supreme Court.

8. Assign a student or small group to make a schedule of upcoming TV and radio broadcasts and films at local cinemas[2] **about** newspapers and journalists. For example: the weekly PBS TV feature, "Frontline," the network "Meet the Press," the PBS regular broadcasts of National Press Club meetings, and local programs, such as Maine Public Broadcasting's weekly TV feature, "Maine Reporter's Notebook," repeated on radio the following day. Post the schedule on the bulletin board.

9. Assign other students to watch or listen to some of the programs listed in the above schedule and to report briefly on them in class.

IX. IS THE PRESS ALWAYS RIGHT?

Historically, the role of the press has been to question authority, but it must not be forgotten that the press itself has often taken a position of authority. After all, the first book Gutenberg printed was that monument of authority, the Bible. The very appearance of words in print lends them a credibility that may not always be justified. The fact that printed words can be stored as a permanent record and the reputations established by well-known newspapers add further credibility to print. The responsibility of the reader

---

[1]Edwin Emery, *The Press and America* (Prentice-Hall, Inc.: Englewood Cliffs, NJ, 1972), pp. 755 and 759

[2]See APPENDIX for titles of related films, books, etc.

to read carefully, analyze, and compare goes hand in hand with the responsibility of the press to provide accurate information. The press is not above question, and often for good reason, as students should have discovered in their research for the history of the newspaper. Criteria for judging newspaper quality are developed in Chapter 1, "Getting Acquainted with the Newspaper," Section VII and ACTIVITIES 17–26.

Some of the most severe criticism of the press comes from within. A panel of well-known journalists speaking at Boston University several years ago cited lazy reporters and incompetent editors for the lack of fresh investigative reporting, said a UPI article. One noted that even the Watergate story was not the result of editorial zeal. "It was kind of sloughed off on two young guys who had a lot of time," said *New York Times* editorial writer Roger Wilkins.

"One of the greatest problems of journalism is that. . .it's run by giant corporations whose leaders. . .don't want to rock the boat," said Ben Bagdikian. Bagdikian, one of the media's severest critics, is the author of *The Media Monopoly*,[1] in which he points out that twenty corporations control more than half the 61 million newspapers sold every day. He charges that interlocking ownership exercises control over the news that gets printed, that editorial content is aimed at the advertisers' market—the affluent readers—and that the newspapers do not serve a large portion of the masses—the young, the elderly, the non-affluent, and the minorities.

Ira Rifkin, a freelance journalist formerly with UPI, scores the "objectivity" of the wire services as nothing more than the blending of conflicting stories into bland, inoffensive, middle-of-the-road reporting.[2]

Just as they must with the news itself, readers must examine criticism from all sides and try to find a balanced perspective.[3]

ACTIVITY

10. Ask students to clip any articles they find anywhere (newspapers, news magazines, other publications) criticizing the media and add them to a file, scrapbook, or bulletin board. If a particularly interesting issue arises, plan some kind of class debate or discussion around it.

X. CHAPTER EVALUATION

In addition to observing students' understanding and response during ACTIVITIES in this chapter, the teacher may wish to use the objective test that follows. Since this guide is intended to be used selectively, it would be impossible to design a test covering all of Part I that would be useful to many readers. If they wish to administer a unit test, teachers should select from tests questions relating to material they have covered.

---

[1] Beacon Press, Boston, 1983. Recommended reading.

[2] Ira Rifkin, "The News Is Wired," *Focus: Media* (San Francisco: Chandler Publishing Co., 1972), pp. 34–40.

[3] **Cross Reference:** Chapter 1, "Getting Acquainted With the Newspaper": X. Criteria for a Good Newspaper

Name _____ Date _____

_____ **OBJECTIVE TEST** _____

*In the blank(s) in each statement, write the letter of the word or phrase that best completes the statement **most** accurately.*

1. There are fewer daily newspapers now than there were in 1910 _____ .

   a. and fewer copies of newspapers are sold every day

   b. but more actual copies of newspapers are printed and sold every day

   c. and circulation has diminished

2. Newspapers _____ compete with television because _____ .

   a. can   c. newspapers provide information not available on TV

   b. cannot   d. people get all the news they need from television

3. Newspapers are _____ the national economy.

   a. not very important in

   b. important only because they provide information to

   c. among the largest manufacturing businesses in

4. One of the most useful characteristics of printed information is that ____ .

   a. it can be stored and referred to again

   b. it's more likely to be true than broadcast information

   c. it's easier to understand than broadcast information

5. The responsibility of the press to investigate activities and people threatening the public interest is known as its _____ role.

   a. detective   b. watchdog   c. propaganda

(continued)

Name _____ Date _____

_____ **OBJECTIVE TEST** _____

(continued)

6. _____ laws to a certain extent protect people from publicity about their private lives.

   a. Libel

   b. Slander

   c. Credibility

7. "Trial by newspaper" _____ .

   a. assures people of getting a fair trial

   b. conflicts with a person's right to a fair trial

   c. is an unquestioned right of the free press

8. _____ guarantee(s) that newspapers can report government proceedings to the people.

   a. Free press laws

   b. The Bill of Rights

   c. Freedom of Access laws

9. News reporters _____ the privilege of protecting their sources of information from legal investigation.

   a. never have

   b. are in some states granted

   c. can count on

10. "Managed news" conflicts with _____ .

    a. the people's right to know

    b. government policy

    c. corporate policy

(continued)

Name _____ Date _____

_____ **OBJECTIVE TEST** _____

(continued)

11. Censorship is _____ .

    a. necessary to protect people from evil

    b. necessary for national security

    c. a continuing threat to freedom of the press

12. The press _____ .

    a. should be able to print anything it wants to

    b. always behaves responsibly

    c. should be responsible for the accuracy and fairness of what it prints

13. Readers should _____ .

    a. take the responsibility of reading and listening to a variety of sources and comparing and analyzing before making up their minds

    b. choose a good newspaper and stick with it

    c. never believe anything they see, read or hear

14. Journalists _____ .

    a. are satisfied with the way the American press operates

    b. are often the severest critics of the press

    c. think everyone is against them

15. _____ of the country's newspapers are owned by big corporations.

    a. More than half

    b. Thirty percent

    c. Only a few

ANSWERS TO
OBJECTIVE TEST

1. b	6. a	11. c
2. a, c	7. b	12. c
3. c	8. c	13. a
4. a	9. b	14. b
5. b	10. a	15. a

XI. SPACE FOR YOUR IDEAS

PART II
The Newspaper as a Tool for Teaching

CHAPTER 9

English

CONTENTS

English

Written communication is the newspaper's major purpose. It is hardly necessary to make a case for the usefulness of written communication in the English classroom. The ACTIVITIES that appear here and the many more you will create from this beginning speak for themselves.

I. READING

Because the newspaper concerns the real world and is recognized as an adult institution, it can be used effectively to motivate older students with reading problems, as well as to improve reading skills at all levels and to provide challenges in critical thinking.

A. COMPREHENSION

ACTIVITIES

1. Basic

1. Select a comic strip. Ask students to read it carefully; then ask questions about the strip. These can be as simple or as sophisticated as necessary, from factual recall to inference.

2. Develop a bulletin board display resembling a newspaper front page, but without headlines. Discuss with the class the problems it presents. Have each student clip five stories with headlines that clearly express the main idea, then cut the headlines from the stories and put all ten pieces in an envelope. Students exchange envelopes and match headlines to proper stories. Ask students to consider the following questions:

   - How does the headline help you to understand the story?

   - Does every headline give a main idea? What other approaches do they take (human interest, humor, catchy wording such as puns or alliteration)? Why?

   - What kinds of words are left out of headlines? Does this prevent you from
   - understanding them? Why are they left out?

- How do the size of type and the number of columns in width affect the wording of headlines?[1]

3. Select an editorial of current interest and develop four or five questions based on it at whatever level is suitable. Photocopy the editorial and questions and distribute them to students. Allow them time for reading and consideration of the questions. Then have students share their observations. Other types of articles may be used for this exercise as well.

4. Provide students with three captions and four pictures from the sports page or from another section of the newspaper. After deciding which captions match the pictures, they can check their choices by reading an uncut copy of the same page.

5. Provide students with a copy of a news story and ask them to write a brief summary of what happened in sequential order. This is not so simple as it sounds. Bear in mind that the inverted pyramid construction is *not* a narrative account.[2]

6. Provide students with copies of a news story and have them write a summary of the main idea. (See also III. Composition, page 164.)

2. Scanning, Skimming, Speeding Up

7. Have students list all the subjects they are taking in their courses this year and scan the newspaper to find examples of information for each. Have them start a file or scrapbook of articles about their favorite subject.

8. Ask students to skim datelines to find items about countries they are studying in other classes. Make a summary of the number of items about the United States, about Canada, and about each continent. Note the distribution.[3]

9. Have students skim for good news and bad news. Discuss in class what each term means. Take a count of items that are predominantly bad news and items that are predominantly good news. Note the proportion. You may wish to have students do this for a week and discuss the results. Ask students, "If you were the editor, would you create a different balance?"

10. Have students skim a sports story to determine what, in their opinion, was the highlight of the game. Ask them to skim to see if there was a turning point and to skim the scoreboard to see how their favorite players are doing.

---

[1]**Cross Reference:** Chapter 2, "What Is News?", box, page 37, and ACTIVITY 15. Adapted from *The Newspaper as an Effective Teaching Tool*, Washington, D.C., the American Newspaper Publishers Association Foundation, 1977, with their permission.

[2]**Cross Reference:** Chapter 2, "What Is News?": III. Inverted Pyramid, and ACTIVITIES 7 and 10

[3]**Cross Reference:** Chapter 11, "Social Studies": II. Geography

11. Make up clues for six articles in different sections of the paper (for example: front page, financial, comics, editorials, sports, entertainment). All students should have copies of the paper if possible. Divide the class into four teams. When the teacher reads a clue, the first student to find the article stands. The team with the most firsts is the winner. Students who do well should explain their strategy, which will doubtless include using the index on the front page.

12. Have students work in pairs. Each student makes up five to ten clues, as in ACTIVITY 11, and times his or her partner's responses. The aim is to get all answers in less time than the partner.

13. Have students scan the paper for commonly used acronyms. Set a short time limit. Discuss the meaning of each acronym.

14. Have students skim restaurant reviews to see which ones they would prefer on the basis of the descriptions. Have them share their findings with classmates.

15. Ask students to skim the TV or movie guide to see what they will watch or go to see in the coming week. Have them make a schedule.

16. Have students scan a feature article in the travel section for colorful words and phrases, underline them, and add them to their vocabulary notebooks. (See also III. Composition, page 164.)

17. Have students scan articles by columnists to find powerful verbs, figures of speech, and other examples of effective writing style. Ask them to underline each and discuss in class. Ask them to add these to their collections, too. (See also II. Language, page 159.)

18. One key to speed reading is fixing the eyes on a group of words rather than on each single word. Have your students draw a line down the center of a story column. Ask them to practice reading the news item by focusing only on that line. Be careful the student does not select a double-width column, such as an editorial.

19. Have students scan the front page or a feature page for ten seconds. Ask each student to list all the things he or she can remember. Doing this frequently will help improve short-term memory and scanning skills.

20. Distribute the daily paper to individual students (or pairs if necessary). Have them turn to a given page in the classified ads and **scan** the page to find cars priced under $1,000 with air conditioning and stick shifts. Repeat with as many different items as you wish. Make this a contest, dividing the class into two or more teams and keeping score.

21. Have students work individually. If there are not enough papers to go around, divide the class and the papers in half, and assign a different article to each half of the class.

Designate an article of appropriate length and difficulty to challenge them. Write three to five questions on the board for each article. Have students skim quickly to find the answers. This may or may not be a contest.

22. Distribute papers as before, but ask students to read the headline of a given article. Then suggest two or three questions it raises, and write them on the board. See how quickly students can skim through the article to find the answers. Repeat with several articles for practice.

23. Have students skim the editorial page to select three interesting editorials. They then set purposes for reading each one, and establish a rate appropriate for the purpose set. Students time each other's reading rate to determine the differences in rate.

24. Have students find and read a legal advertisement to stretch their comprehension skills. They should then write a short paragraph describing the main idea of the advertisement. Discuss why this kind of ad is necessary.[1]

B. LITERATURE

ACTIVITIES

25. The conflict and drama of real life that constitute news are also the essence of good fiction. Have the class discuss several news and human interest stories in the daily paper as possible material for a short story or novel. Ask them to identify characters, plot, setting, theme, and mood. You might wish to carry the idea into written individual assignments, with each student finding an article of interest and outlining suggestions for a story based on it.[2]

26. Reverse the above ACTIVITY, and have students write a straight news inverted-pyramid-style story or a human interest feature (whichever is more suitable), based on a short story or an incident in a novel they are currently reading. A class discussion comparing results should not only clarify any misunderstandings, but also reveal possibilities for various interpretations.[3]

27. Have students develop a newspaper for a period of literature they are studying (for example: a Victorian newspaper if they are reading *Great Expectations* or a Roman newspaper if they are reading *Julius Caesar*). They can have fun developing a nameplate, editorials, cartoons, etc., as well as news stories.[4]

[1]**Cross Reference:** Chapter 11, "Social Studies": IV. Sociology/Anthropology

[2]**Cross Reference:** Chapter 2, "What Is News?": News Values. Adapted from *The Newspaper as an Effective Teaching Tool*, Washington, D.C., the American Publishers Association Foundation, 1977, with their permission.

[3]*Ibid.*, III. Inverted Pyramid and ACTIVITY 7.

[4]**Cross Reference:** Chapter 7, "News and History": ACTIVITY 2

28. Have students write obituaries for famous literary characters.[1]

29. To help students identify settings, ask them to describe the setting of their favorite comic strip.

30. To help students understand the personal and political conflicts that led to the assassination of Julius Caesar (and to its parallels throughout history), have students research the political situation around recent assassinations. Subsequent discussion will illustrate the relationships between the incidence of violence and the use and abuse of political power. It should also reveal Shakespeare's perceptive powers and the way his language sharpens these insights.

    Questions for students to consider:

    - What were the motivations of Caesar, Brutus, Cassius, Mark Antony? Was each hoping for personal gain, for political gain, or for both? Answer the same questions about a recent assassination.

    - Is it easy to identify the "right" or "wrong" protagonists in a conflict that leads to assassination?

    - Did the people in these conflicts seem to act independently or were they influenced to act in ways they might not have chosen on their own?

    - What are the major reasons an individual or group feels justified in taking a political leader's life? Could these reasons ever justify such action to you? Think about the unsuccessful attempt to assassinate Hitler during World War II. Was that attempt justified?

    - What solutions to orderly political change other than assassination work better? Considering human nature, is it possible to resist the use of force? Do you think you and others can make the future less violent?

    - Is Shakespeare's play so vivid that you can sense the feelings of hope, anger, and fear that are present when a leader is assassinated? How does Shakespeare convey these feelings?

    To demonstrate their understanding, have students write and produce a short play enacting a recent assassination. The dialogue and actions should reflect the conclusions reached in discussing the above questions.[2] (See IV. Oral English, page 173.)

31. When reading poetry about working people, such as Walt Whitman's "I Hear America Singing" or Carl Sandburg's "Chicago," ask students to illustrate the poem with classified ads.

32. Use the comics to help students identify various literary concepts such as melodrama, romance, satire, comedy, irony, fantasy, myth, science fiction (just about

---

[1]**Cross Reference:** Chapter 5, "Sports, Comics, and Other Special Features": ACTIVITY 36
[2]**Cross Reference:** Chapter 11, "Social Studies." Adapted from *The Newspaper as an Effective Teaching Tool*, Washington, D.C., the American Publishers Association Foundation, 1977, with their permission.

everything but tragedy—and enough of that can be found on other pages of the newspaper); and stock character types like the mythic hero and heroine, the demonic enemy, the siren, the tyrant, *miles gloriosus* (the bragging soldier), the gullible bumpkin, the wily peasant, the scapegoat. While these may be simply stereotypes in the comics, they can often clarify the meaning of such terminology.

33. Use the comics to illustrate various types of humor, such as satire, the pun, slapstick, wit, irony, and sight gags. Make, or have students make, a bulletin board display.

34. Irony, contrast, and surprise are all elements of humor. Have students find examples of each of them in the newspaper.

C. CRITICAL THINKING

ACTIVITIES

35. Have students read a feature story and summarize in their own words what they consider its most important aspect. In a class discussion, have students share their views.

36. Provide students with copies of a provocative editorial. Divide the class into two groups to discuss the pros and cons of the writer's position. (See also IV. Oral English, page 173.)

37. Have students read a feature story, locate details, and classify them as a) important, b) helpful, and c) unnecessary, as they relate to the main idea.

38. Have students, either individually or in groups, read a news feature about a current controversy and make a prediction of possible future events, based on facts in the story and logical inferences. After a period of several weeks, have them check their predictions against what has actually developed.

39. Using a news story of interest to students, have them discuss the causes for the occurrences and the effects those causes had on the incident or people involved.

40. Assign the writing of an imaginary dialogue or interview between two people who might be considered incongruous. The purpose is to create awareness of personal bias or point of view regarding social pressures or news of the day (e.g., Walter Cronkite and Robin Williams; Jacqueline Onassis and Little Orphan Annie; Funky Winkerbean and your school principal). (See also III. Creative Writing, page 167.)*

---

*Cross Reference: Chapter 11, "Social Studies": IV. Sociology/Anthropology

II. LANGUAGE

A. SEMANTICS

ACTIVITIES

41. Have students select any classified ad and replace as many of the words as possible with synonyms. Then have them find another ad and replace as many words as possible with antonyms.

42. Have students collect and mount ten headlines with negative words in them. Ask them to underline the negative words and to substitute at least two synonyms for each. In class discussion, have students share the most interesting changes of meaning that result.

43. To emphasize the impact of words, have students underline the superlatives and the kinds of words found in advertising and headlines. Start a collection of descriptive words found in the newspaper such as those describing sound (gurgle, chuckle, etc.), image words (slump, straggling, foundering, etc.), color words (white-hot, azure, ruby, flaming, etc.), and words that emphasize (overwhelm, emblazon, etc.).

44. Have students clip and mount a news story of at least five paragraphs. Their assignment is to underline all the facts in red and all the opinions in green. Students should share their findings in a class discussion.

45. Have students go through an article and circle all words with positive connotations, regardless of context. Do the same for words with negative connotations. Class members should compare lists and discuss any disagreements.

46. Using the same article as above, or another, substitute words with the same meaning, but the opposite connotation. Discuss how this alters the slant, if not the meaning, of the article.

47. Have students scan the sports pages and list as many ways as they can find to say "won" or "lost." What other words can they find in the newspaper that are synonyms or antonyms?

48. From the Sunday funnies to Shakespeare, the **pun** or **equivocation**, with its element of incongruity, is the essence of wit. Most puns are verbal, based on homonyms—words that look or sound alike, or almost alike, but that have different meanings. Some puns are visual rather than verbal. Have students find examples of both verbal and visual puns in the comics and mount them for a bulletin board display.

49. Comic strips use **stereotypes** to a great extent. Discuss this with students and have them find examples for a bulletin board display.

50. Letters to the editor are often written by angry people who are not trained to be objective. Have students find examples of stereotypes in letters to the editor. Some may be interesting enough to use in a bulletin board display.

51. Editorial cartoons, in their use of satire and caricature, also use the device of stereotyping to get their idea across. Have students examine several editorial cartoons and discuss whether their use of stereotyping is justified in any way, or whether they are completely unfair.*

52. How do newspaper advertisements show male-female stereotyping? Have students examine several ads in today's newspaper. Ask them to determine toward whom the ad is directed. How many men are shown in the ads? How many women? What kind of products or services appear to be associated with each? What kind of conclusions can students draw from evidence suggested by the ads? Are these conclusions accurate?

53. Advertising makes use of all the common **propaganda devices**. Have students clip and mount examples of:

    – Glittering generalities

    – Transfer (glamor, authority, intelligence, other "virtues" by association)

    – Testimonial

    – Plainfolks

    – Card stacking (slanting by selection, distraction, false logic)

    – Bandwagon ("everybody's doing it")

    – Appeal to science, status

54. Have students study the persuasive words used in ads and make a collection of the most interesting ones. Have them write an advertisement selling themselves, choosing their words carefully to present the best possible image.

55. Have students find examples of **slang**, **idiom**, and **dialect** in the comics. Why are these used? Is this a useful or a harmful practice? Explain. Find similar examples in other parts of the newspaper. Are they used for the same purposes as in comics?

---

*Cross Reference:** Chapter 8, "The Newspaper Today": III. Libel

B. FIGURATIVE LANGUAGE

ACTIVITIES

56. **Onomatopoeia** is an alarming word for many students. The newspaper can help them become familiar with its meaning. Divide the class into teams and set a time limit for finding as many words as possible in the daily newspaper that sound like what they are describing. The comics are a good place to start, but insist that a certain portion must come from other pages, so they will realize that onomatopoeia is ubiquitous. (See also non-verbal symbols for sounds, ACTIVITY 70, page 164.)

57. Taking the cue from the comics, have students create illustrations to accompany some of the more interesting sound words they discover. Post these on the bulletin board.

58. Have students add a list of onomatopoeic words to their notebooks to use when writing both prose and poetry.

59. Ask students to make a collection of words found in the newspaper, 25 verbs and 25 nouns, that express or describe the five senses.

60. Students will be surprised to find that even the musical devices of language can be found in the newspaper as well as in literature. The most obvious one of these is **alliteration**, a favorite with headline writers, often to the point of excess. But they can also find many examples of **consonance** and **assonance**, and occasionally even rhyme, in the newspaper. Divide the class into teams for a scavenger hunt. They are to find:

    - Five headlines that use alliteration

    - Three examples of alliteration not in headlines

    - Three examples of consonance anywhere

    - Three examples of assonance anywhere

    - At least one deliberate rhyme

    - Bonus point for an unintentional rhyme

61. One of the easiest ways to acquaint students with the concept of **metaphor** is to demonstrate the absurdity of taking the meaning literally. (And incidentally, teach the meaning of the word "literally," which often escapes students, at the same time.) Have students find a comic or cartoon in which the artist has made a joke of taking a metaphor literally.

62. Have students create their own cartoons, for display on the bulletin board, illustrating a metaphor or simile, for example: "It's raining cats and dogs."

63. Provide students with copies of an interesting feature story and have them choose appropriate phrases to rewrite as metaphors or similes.

64. Ask students to find three metaphors and three similes on the sports page. Next ask them to find three more of each anywhere else in the newspaper. Which was easier?

65. **Mixed metaphors** come in all sizes and degrees of capacity to amuse. The best ones find their way to the *New Yorker*. Offer a small reward for the most humorous example of a mixed metaphor to be found in the daily paper in a week's time. (*Hint:* Letters to the Editor and speeches of politicians are good places to start looking.) See also the article on page 163.

66. **Hyperbole**, like other colorful language, is easiest to find on the sports pages, especially in the headlines. Have students find three examples on the sports pages and three anywhere else in the paper. Again, discuss the ease or difficulty they encountered in finding examples.

67. **Personification** is another figure of speech used frequently in the newspaper. Have students find visual examples in cartoons and comics. The next step is for them to find verbal personifications. The best place to start is the editorial page, where eloquence may invoke the device. Another place to look is in accounts of political speeches in news articles.

68. **Allegory** is frequently used in comics. One of the best examples was the now-extinct "Pogo," which was not about animals living in a swamp at all. "Pogo" was the source of the famous line, "We have met the enemy and he is US." Ask students to try to find an example of allegory in the comics of their daily paper.

69. **Symbols** are a vital aspect of communication.* Verbal symbolism can be simple or extremely complex. After a discussion of symbols, have students find examples in the newspaper. You may wish to accept both verbal and non-verbal symbols as one exercise, or limit them to one kind at a time. In any case, they should become aware of both.

---

*See S.I. Hayakawa, *Language in Thought and Action* (New York: Harcourt Brace & World, 1964).

The following article, originally printed in the *Los Angeles Times*,
is reprinted by permission of the author.

Take metaphors out of journalism's sails

Nancy Nelson

Commentary

A crumbling structure, or a severe case of hardening arteries? The press has described the world economic situation using both metaphors. These simple but clever images, however, are not as innocent as we might assume: The repeated use of figurative language by journalists can subtly shape public perspectives. This has profound implications for objectivity and the power of the press.

Metaphors are a fundamental part of our conceptual system. We could not eliminate them from our vocabulary or our press. They are necessary for communication. Nevertheless, metaphor is never objective; it is rhetorical. And by framing an issue in a particular way, metaphors reinforce certain social values. For example, mainstream newspapers tend to use metaphors that reflect a culture's dominant values, while conservative or radical papers choose metaphors that stress alternatives.

This lack of objectivity is especially apparent in the economic metaphors found in the press. For example, the New York Times discusses the economic situation as a health problem: The World Economic Body Has a Circulatory Malady. This focus is evidenced in quotes such as "...policy directives that get to the heart of the domestic economy ...." (May 31). The illness is referred to as an "epidemic of recession" or a "planetary ailment," and in one case is given this diagnosis: "Drastic upheavals in the circulatory system of the world's economic body left deep scars like a heart attack" (Sept. 7).

Recovery from this malady requires free circulation, which should stimulate growth and a healthy body. This is implied when the Times says that "the catch is cash flow and the cure is sound programs..." (Sept. 14) and "...the world economy grows when trade grows" (Oct. 18).

Leftist publications discuss the world economy quite differently. In their metaphorical language the world economy is a crumbling structure. They imply that the the principles on which the economy was built are unstable. Said the Guardian on Nov. 17, 1982: "Now with the whole interdependent structure somewhat wobbly...." The Workers World last May 6: "A default would rock the foundations of the capitalist banking fraternity."

These papers insinuate that reconstruction must ultimately rest on a sound foundation. Workers World noted that Marx's solution is the "undoing of capitalism and construction upon its ashes...(of) a new order." The difference between these metaphors corresponds to the different political and economic orientations of the newspapers that use them. The New York Times' emphasis on the system's circulation and maintenance suggests our own capitalist economy. Our understanding of the issue is shaped by this organic image. Survival is the primary concern. The body is in our image; it cannot die.

Metaphors generate their own solutions, and actions that fit within the definitions, inferences and limits of these metaphors are sanctioned by them. For example, the circulation malady requires free circulation and the removal of any blockages to monetary flow—which is also the "cure" that the Reagan administration has "prescribed."

Elsewhere, the problems of Central America are referred to as falling objects—dominoes—some of which must be supported and others destabilized.

Newsweek (June 6) discusses the "pressures which will set off another earthquake in Managua, toppling the hard-line leftists." Other publications describe the region as a quagmire, in which we sink deeper and deeper. The June issue of Mother Jones features "scenes of El Salvador where President Reagan has mired the U.S." And the Guardian (May 11) refers to "the Reagan administration's sinking into the new 'Big Muddy' of Central America."

Nuclear armament, and the MX missile in particular, are similarly portrayed by metaphors that reflect opposing ideologies.

The mainstream press depicts a competitive game. For the Times of India (April 5) it is a race: "The Soviets tend to follow the American lead in the arms race, but they always catch up." Newsweek (June 6) describes a poker game: "The most common and effective argument against the MX as a bargaining chip is simply that $15 billion is a little steep for any poker hand."

In contrast, the leftist press uses science-fiction to suggest the "monstrousness" of nuclear armament. The Nation (April 16) called it "the new weapons Frankenstein," and the Guardian (April 20) headlined: "MX basing plan: From absurdity to madness."

Metaphors, as we can see, are rhetorically powerful—especially when they are used by the press. And the press influences many people. With metaphors it can implicitly sanction some actions over others while still claiming objectivity. We must recognize that, with figurative language, objectivity is not possible. Metaphors are manipulative tools.

Nancy Nelson is a graduate student in anthropology at the University of New Mexico.

The Los Angeles Times

C. NON–VERBAL LANGUAGE

ACTIVITIES

70. **Symbols** of all kinds can be found in the newspaper. Divide the class into teams, and ask them to scan the daily paper for as many non-verbal symbols as they can find: mathematical, scientific, printer's, sounds (in the comics), visual in photos and ads, etc. In order to qualify, a symbol must be explained by the team members. This may even involve a bit of research.

71. Another kind of **non-verbal language** to be found in the newspaper is **body language**. Have students begin with the comics and collect drawings that express emotions such as fear, anger, surprise, joy, sorrow. Note any that use other parts of the body than the face to convey the emotion. How do they know which emotion is being expressed?

72. Repeat the above ACTIVITY using photos in the paper. Discuss the differences they discover in identifying the emotions expressed (if any).

III. WRITING

A. COMPOSITION

ACTIVITIES

1. Classification, Outlining, Organization

73. Have students work in pairs. Each student cuts out five to ten classified ads and challenges his or her partner to determine the **classification** under which each was found.

74. Have each student cut fifteen classified ads out of the paper and put them into an envelope. Exchange envelopes. Now each student must arrange the ads in his or her envelope in **alphabetical** order and paste them on a sheet of construction paper.

75. To strengthen understanding of chronological **sequence**, provide pictures from a news page and have students determine which pictures illustrate the same event. They then arrange them in a logical order and use them to write a news story.

76. Another sequence exercise that's not so easy as it looks, sometimes, is to cut cartoons into separate frames and have students put them into proper sequence.

77. For practice in **paraphrasing**, have students read an article, develop an outline, then write a summary from the outline. Finally, have them compare it with the actual article.

78. **Organizational skills** can be honed by having students work with the week-long TV schedule. They may choose one category (such as sports, music, drama, science, or news specials) and make a viewing schedule for themselves for the week.

79. To give students practice in **organizing** main ideas and supporting details in outline format, divide the class into groups. Give all members of a group copies of the same news story. Students work individually to identify what each feels to be the most important idea in each paragraph. In the group they discuss these ideas, find support in the article, and put their findings into an outline.

80. Writing classified ads helps students to focus on essentials as for *précis* writing and to choose words that give as much **specific information** as possible. Have students write a classified ad. Use as few words as possible without leaving out any information. Remember, you are being charged for every word. Read some of today's classified ads for examples.* (See also page 166.)

2. Expository Writing

81. The following will give you some ideas for expository writing assignments:

Chapter 4, "The Editorial Pages": III. Writing Editorials; IV. Guidelines for Writing Editorials, ACTIVITIES 9–11; VII. Letters to the Editor, ACTIVITIES 20–22; Chapter 3, "Features": III. How to Write Features, ACTIVITIES 9–13; V. Reviews, ACTIVITIES 14–16; Chapter 2, "What Is News?": IV. Writing a News Story, ACTIVITY 12; Chapter 5, "Sports, Comics, and Other Special Features": VI. Writing Your Own Sports Story.

82. Students will be likely to put greater effort into **expository writing** when it is related to the real world through the newspaper. Have them read the jobs listed in the help-wanted sections of the classified ads. They should choose one they would like to have and write a letter of application, describing their qualifications. The ad should be attached to the letter.

83. Use the newspaper as a springboard for **letter writing**. Students can write letters to Dear Abby or Ann Landers, letters of application for jobs advertised in the classifieds, letters to the editor, and the like.

84. For practice in **description**, have students select a comic strip character and describe him or her in words. They should include physical characteristics, occupation, personality, family, home, etc.

---

*Cross Reference: Chapter 6, "Advertising": IV. Writing Your Own Ads, ACTIVITIES 6-9. Reprinted by permission of the Canadian Daily Newspaper Publishers Association.

CLASSIFIED ADVERTISEMENTS
(The *Précis*)

1. My wife and I are very happy about an event in our family recently. My wife, whose name is Dale, give birth to a baby. This occurred at Grace Hospital. The baby is a girl and we have named her Stephany Violet. Incidentally, my first name is Stanley. Stephany weighed 6 lbs. 4 oz. at birth, but, of course, we expect she'll put on weight as she grows. She was born on August 2, 1979. My last name is Wilson. *(Ad contains 26 words)*

2. My dad says he's heard enough of my 1969 motorbike. I have decided discretion is the better part of valor and I'm going to sell it before he goes right through the ceiling. I'm sorry to see it go because I've partly customized it and it has many extra parts. It is a Triumph. I hope to get $1,000 for it, but I don't really think I will. My telephone number is 945-2579 if you're interested. *(13 words)*

3. I have a 1955 car, believe it or not. It is not exactly in what you would call mint condition. In fact, it needs a little work to put it in satisfactory shape. It's a Chevy. I'll take whatever I can get for it. I hope to get $250. My name is Richard but my friends call me Rick. If you want to buy this car call me at 948-9867 at 7 p.m. Oh yes, the car has two doors. *(18 words)*

4. If you were a retired teacher as I am and had this old desk around, what would you do with it? Sell it? That's what I'm hoping to do. I want $15 for it. It comes with a chair. Of course, if I can't get $15 for it, I'll take what I can get. Call me at 256-9074. *(9 words)*

5. There are three of us children, see? Our father's name is Daddy. Our names are Kara, John, and Edward. Of course, that lets the cat out of the bag and you recognize us now, don't you? Well, we just wanted to wish you a happy birth, Ma Squaw. And we would like to say we love you. *(12 words)*

6. I wish now I had put Angel's tags on her before I put her out in the yard. Well, no use crying over spilt milk. She's gone. But I want her back. You would want your German shepherd back, wouldn't you? She disappeared near George Avenue and Tecumseh. If you have found her, please call me at 945-8241. *(15 words)*

85. For a short expository writing assignment, ask students to write a paragraph about their favorite cartoon character. Have them present a convincing argument for their choice.

86. **Interpreting** editorial cartoons is a good expository writing project. Ask students to examine the editorial cartoon in today's paper and to write a short statement explaining the cartoonist's point of view.

87. Find three house-for-sale ads that list both price and square feet of living area. Have the class figure the price per square foot for each. Then have students write a paragraph that beings: "It is helpful to know the number of square feet of living space in a house because. . ."[1]

88. Find in the classified section the notice to job applicants regarding Title VII of the Civil Rights Act. Have each student write an explanation of what it means. Have students attach the statement from the newspaper to their papers.[2]

89. Book reviews are also expository writing. The accompanying guide (R) for writing book reviews (reports) should be helpful (see page 168).

3. Creative Writing

90. While most newspaper writing does not fall into the category popularly regarded as "creative," such as fiction and poetry, the **starters for creative writing** to be found in the newspaper are endless. The comics are a good place to begin. Have students retell the story in a favorite comic strip. They will have to provide details of setting, facial expressions, and movements.

91. Have students choose a comic strip character and make up their own story for a future episode (one that has not appeared in the strip). Remind them that the character's actions and reactions must be consistent with his or her established character.

92. Select a simple cartoon. White out the dialogue in the balloons and photocopy. Have students create their own **dialogue** for the characters.

93. For further practice in writing dialogue, have students write a story using the characters and words from a comic strip. Remind them they will have to use good descriptive words, since the reader will not be able to see the drawing.

94. A simple exercise in **plot** development is to have students select a comic strip that tells a continuing story and predict what tomorrow's episode will be. Have them check tomorrow's newspaper to see how accurate the prediction was.

---

[1]**Cross Reference:** Chapter 13, "Math"

[2]**Cross Reference:** Chapter 11, "Social Studies": Sociology; Chapter 15, "Career Education"

GUIDELINES FOR WRITING REVIEWS: BOOK, FILM, TELEVISION

1. *Do NOT tell the story.* Instead, give a brief summary of the main idea and what you consider to be the author's purpose in writing the story, book, film, or TV script.

2. *Choose the thing that impressed you most,* preferably favorably, but if necessary, unfavorably. (Be honest!) Basically, did the work succeed in doing what the author apparently set out to do? Concentrate on this point, and support your comment by direct references to the text. Here you may relate details of certain incidents to make your point clear. For example:

    - *Characterization:* individual, as written by the author *and*, for film and TV, as interpreted by the actors and director.

    - *Plot Structure:* Does it give a convincing picture of reality? Is this achieved by linear or non-linear means or both?

    - *Fairness:* Does the work give a balanced or a biased view? If biased, is there a good reason for it? In the case of non-fiction books and documentary films and TV, is the point of view objective or subjective? Can the author's (director's) position be justified?

    - *"The medium is the message":* How does the method of presentation—writing style, camera, and acting techniques—help to create the impression you get?

3. *Be objective yourself.* Although a review is a statement of your own opinion, it should be a fair look at the book, film, or TV show. Be sure to mention good or bad points that contrast with your main point.

4. *Write in standard essay style.* Do NOT take up the above points in the order given or list them numerically. Simply *keep them in mind* and include them as appropriate in a well-written essay. A well-written essay has an *opening paragraph* where you state your main thesis, four or five paragraphs in which you both develop your main point with supporting evidence and offer contrasting points, and a *closing paragraph* in which you summarize your main point.

    Depending on the circumstances, use the first person (I) for a fairly informal situation, or the third person if the requirements are more formal or academic.

5. Finally, *do read published reviews* to get an idea of their style.

95. Have students select a favorite comic strip and rewrite it as a short story. Remind them they will have to describe the setting and action, as there will be no pictures. Be sure to use correct form for quotations in writing dialogue.

96. **Classified ads** also make good **story starters**. In the Lost and Found section, have students choose an ad for a lost item and write a story in the first person, telling about what happened to it.

97. Ask students to select an animal from the Pets section and to write a story about its life after it is bought or adopted by someone.

98. Students should work in pairs for this one. Have them find a classified ad that they think has an interesting story behind it. Then ask them to discuss what might have happened before and after the ad was placed. One person writes the "before" story, and the other writes the "after" story.

99. Have students select an ad from the Articles for Sale section and write a humorous story about why the owner wants to sell this item.

100. Choose a human interest story and have students write a story about what they think happened before and/or after the events reported in the story. Comparing different students' versions should be fun and instructive. Discuss how given facts control the possibilities to some extent.

101. Have students find a news story with an unhappy ending and rewrite it with a happy ending. They may change any details necessary to achieve the desired outcome.

102. Turning to the sports page, have students find a story about a major upset and write a first-person story from the **point of view** of:
    – The star of the winning team
    – The coach of the winning team
    – The player on the losing team whose error caused the upset
    – The coach of the losing team

103. Find enough newspaper photos that could be the basis of a story for every member of the class. Clip and mount and place in a large shopping bag. Ask each student to draw one and write a story about what happened before the picture was taken and what will happen later. No fair swapping.

104. Have students find a newspaper story involving people in conflict. Have them write a story in which they develop the characters of the participants in a plausible way.

105. Have students find a news story with a theme of tragic love, violence, revenge, or adventure and write a ballad about it. Those who wish to may set it to music. Discuss how such ballads were once the news stories of the day.

106. After reading an article about a scientific event, such as a space shot or an eclipse, have students write a science fiction story based on the event.[1]

107. Just for fun, have students cut words and phrases from several **different** headlines. Ask students to paste them on a sheet of paper to form a new, silly headline and to write the story to go with the headline.

108. Have students collect interesting phrases from headlines. These should be dropped into a box or paper bag. Have each student draw one and write a **short poem** that incorporates the phrase.

109. Have students read a news or feature story that interests them. Next they must draw and cut out an appropriate shape (a tree, a globe, an animal, a rocket, etc.) from the newsprint itself. Have them paste the shape on a sheet of paper and examine the words contained in it. By underlining certain words, they will form an **"instant" concrete poem**. This may be carried a step further by having them rearrange the words to compose a poem outside the confines of the shape.

B. GRAMMAR

ACTIVITIES

1. Sentence Structure

110. The Five Ws can make an instructive grammar lesson. Have students find lead paragraphs that contain clear-cut examples of the Five Ws.[2] Have them try to identify which part of the sentence each W presents.

Example:

| where | who | | why |

BATH — A Navy pilot who died in a rescue mission in Vietnam in

| what | | how |

1965 will be remembered in the naming of a guided missile frigate which will be launched by Bath Iron Works following a noon cere-

| when |

mony Saturday.

 – Who—subject
 – (does) What—verb

---

[1]**Cross Reference:** Chapter 12, "Science"

[2]**Cross Reference:** Chapter 2, "What Is News?": II. Summary Lead, ACTIVITIES 5 and 6

- When—adverb modifier
- Where—(dateline) If there were no dateline, the place would have to be mentioned in the paragraph. If the last line read "**at Bath Iron Works**" (place) rather than "**by Bath Iron Works**" (company), Bath Iron Works would be the "where."
- Why—adjective clause modifying subject.

Do the Five Ws perform the same functions in every summary lead sentence?

111. Use the newspaper as a **drill sheet for grammar study**. Have students find and circle verbs, nouns (proper and common), adjectives, adverbs, prepositional phrases, dependent clauses, etc. This is usually more fun than working with sentences in an English book, and it is often a lot more challenging. Both teacher and students will find that the language of the real world is a bit different from that in grammar lessons.

112. To review **parts of speech**, have students collect ten headlines and underline all the verbs in red, all the nouns in green. What parts of speech are usually missing from headlines? (Articles, conjunctions; often adjectives, adverbs)

113. Using the same headlines or others, have students write them as complete sentences. Draw their attention to the fact that headlines are actually kernel sentences.[1]

114. For further illustration of the importance of each element in a sentence, try this puzzle. Take four articles of three or four paragraphs each. Remove the verbs from one, leaving underlined blanks, the nouns from another, the modifiers from the third, and articles from the fourth. Provide each student with a copy of all four articles. Ask students to rewrite each article by filling in each blank with an appropriate word. When they're through, pass out copies of the original articles. There will be some surprises. For an extra good class, you can make this tougher by not leaving any blanks to fill in. This will come even closer to the kinds of sentences teachers sometimes find on student papers, and show them how the other half suffers! Discuss the following questions:

- Which of the four articles was hardest to reconstruct?

- Which part of speech most gives a sentence its meaning?

- Have students examine all types of newspaper material, from news to comics. Is the importance of a part of speech changed by the style and purpose of the article?

SUGGESTION: When marking student stories, underline all the correct sentences in green, rather than the incorrect ones in red. They'll appreciate the positive approach.[2]

[1] **Cross Reference:** See Chapter 2, "What Is News?": V. Headlines

[2] Adapted from *The Newspaper as an Effective Teaching Tool*, Washington, D.C., the American Newspaper Publishers Association Foundation, 1977, with their permission.

2. Punctuation

115. Journalists make mistakes. Ask students to review today's newspaper to **find errors in spelling, grammar, and punctuation**. Some are actually typographical errors. The writers really know how to spell most words. Punctuation rules differ, too. Check the Associated Press or United Press International stylebook (see BIBLIOGRAPHY). For example, newspaper style does not put a comma after the last word in a series before "and." Some of the more ridiculous errors are those of word division. Not all typesetting computers are sophisticated enough to divide words properly, which causes such end-of-line word divisions as eig-ht and th-en. Checking up on the professionals will sharpen student skills.

116. Provide all students with copies of a short article and have them locate **punctuation** marks. They must rewrite the article, using different marks in each instance. Working in small groups, have them note how much meaning has been changed by changing the punctuation.

117. The classified ads are full of **abbreviations**. Have students make a list of abbreviations that are peculiar to help-wanted ads, to house ads, to car ads, to personals. Ask them to explain each abbreviation.

118. Have the class choose an editorial in the daily paper. Have each student rewrite it, using **contractions** in as many places as possible. They then share the results, comparing the effectiveness of the two writing styles.

C. VOCABULARY

ACTIVITIES

119. Have students develop a **vocabulary** notebook, using unfamiliar words they encounter in their daily newspaper reading. They should cut out the sentence containing the word, underline the word, and accompany each entry with a definition.

    Have students find as many acronyms as possible in the newspaper and find out what each stands for.

120. Have students find and clip ten plural words from the newspaper. These should be pasted on plain paper and the root word written beside each plural form. A more sophisticated task would be to have them find ten words that form their plurals by some other means than adding **s**, paste them up, and write the singular form beside each. (They might even learn to sort out criterion–criteria and phenomenon–phenomena.)

121. Have students skim a newspaper page for words that are used with more than one meaning. Have them clip and mount the sentences containing these words and write a definition (checked with a dictionary) for each.

122. On the sports page, have students underline all the words that mean (for example) "hired" and check their selections by interchanging the words to see if the meaning remains the same.

123. A small contest: in five minutes, how many pairs of **homonyms** can students find in today's newspaper?

124. Give students a list of **prefixes** and have them locate words with these prefixes in a news story. The assignment is to substitute a word or phrase for each, without changing the meaning of the sentence.

125. Have students create a crossword puzzle from words in a newspaper story, checking the dictionary for understanding of the words.

126. Pass out copies of a feature article in which every tenth word has been crossed out. Students must fill in the blanks with **words appropriate** to the context and share the results with a partner.

127. Cartoons and comics often contain **words that are new** to students. Have them keep a vocabulary notebook of these words. Using the cartoons as illustrations can make the notebook more attractive and more motivating.

128. **Neologism** is a term that students might not recognize, but they will be interested that new words are being created all the time. Ask students to find examples of words in today's newspaper that are not in the classroom dictionary. They must look them up and *not* find them there to prove they are right.

IV. ORAL ENGLISH

ACTIVITIES

129. Working in groups, have students reduce the front page of today's newspaper to a one-minute **news broadcast**. Have them take turns reading it while one student times them. Use a tape recorder if possible.*

130. From an account they read on the sports page, have students develop a "radio broadcast" of the game or event.

*****Cross Reference:** Chapter 8, "The Newspaper Today": I. Have Radio and Television Made Newspapers Obsolete? ACTIVITIES 2–4

131. Have students clip a newspaper article about a conflict and then research the story to find the causes. They should list what each party to the conflict is doing. Have students choose sides to support and participate in a **debate** on the subject. They must be sure to back up their arguments with factual statements.

132. Have students choose an editorial and develop from it a **persuasive** speech to present to the class.

133. To improve **oral interpretation**, have students take turns reading the comics to the class each day, emphasizing expressive skills.

134. Have students choose a comic strip that tells a continuing story and collect daily episodes over a period of time. When they have sufficient material, have them write a **play** about the story and perform it.

V. SPACE FOR YOUR IDEAS

The Arts

CONTENTS

The Arts

I. THE PERFORMING ARTS

The newspaper's most valuable application in the area of the performing arts is to provide information and background on programs and artists. Teachers of drama, music, and dance can help students make the connection between their own enthusiasms and the world "out there" by involving them in small projects and informal discussions that keep them informed but do not become burdensome.

ACTIVITIES

1. Have students use information from the daily paper to develop an attractive bulletin board in your class or rehearsal room, rotating responsibility on a regular basis. The display should include:

   - A weekly schedule of live stage, radio, and television performances available in your area (including ticket prices)

   - Announcements of summer events (festivals abound) in your area or in areas students may be visiting

   - Reviews of recent performances, including their own

   - Columns written on the arts

   - News and feature stories about local and national artists

   - Stories about the students themselves that appear in local papers

   - Background features on their areas of the arts

   - Articles about career possibilities in their fields

   - Advertisements of contests and competitions they might enter

2. Encourage students to use the schedule (which must be kept up to date to be useful) to attend live performances, either on their own or in groups organized by class members.

3. Call attention to special-interest publications on the performing arts—such as *Variety* (national), the *Boston Phoenix* (regional), *Sweet Potato* (local in Maine and northern Massachusetts)—and keep current copies available.

4. Allow some time in class or afterward for discussion of news and reviews that arouse students' interest (or indignation!). Help them to understand that reviewers are not always experts and that their criticism represents a personal perception, even when it is balanced. Although reviewers often provide fresh insights that can be used constructively, their reviews must be examined carefully for evidence of bias or lack of information and can sometimes be dismissed entirely. This kind of (lifelong!) assurance is especially necessary for serious students planning careers in performance.

5. Ask English and journalism teachers to include performances in your subject area as review assignments, and help students to develop the necessary insights for writing them.[1] (In most cases, it would be unfair for performing arts teachers to assign written reviews. Getting away from the desk and into action is, after all, the main reason for being a performer.)

6. For ideas from the newspaper to spark improvisations and the writing of original plays, see Chapter 9, "English": III. Writing, ACTIVITIES 90–106 for story starters and IV. Oral English, ACTIVITIES 133 and 134.

II. VISUAL ARTS

A. GRAPHICS AND DESIGN

The newspaper itself is the world's most widely disseminated example of graphic design, for better or for worse. A collection of newspapers can illustrate a wide variety of graphic styles as well as provide examples, both outstanding and embarrassing.[2]

ACTIVITIES

7. Use a pile of old newspapers as a source for examples you might need, such as different type faces and their uses.

8. Have students clip newspaper ads that illustrate points you make about graphic design.

9. Have students design display advertisements, using newspaper ads as models.

10. Have students participate in the ad design contest sponsored by local newspapers in many areas during National Newspaper in Education Week (early March).

---

[1]**Cross Reference:** Chapter 3, "Features": VI. Hints for Reviewing Performances; Chapter 9, "English": III. Writing—Guidelines for Writing Reviews

[2]**Cross Reference:** Chapter 2, "What Is News?": VI. Layout, ACTIVITY 16

11. Use editorial cartoons from the daily paper to illustrate the graphic arts legacy of Goya, Daumier, Hogarth, Cruikshank, Nast, *et al.*

12. Have students study editorial cartoons and create their own, focusing on a school, local, or national issue.

13. Have students compare newspaper photos of political figures with various cartoonists' renditions to discover how they achieve their caricatures. Which ones do they think are most effective? Why? Have them create an original caricature of a political figure. Ask them not to imitate a syndicated cartoon.

14. Have students collect their favorite comic strips and analyze the graphic techniques that make them successful.[1]

15. Have students create their own comic strips.

16. Discuss with students earlier forms of newspaper illustration, before photography was used. Have them make a display of the development from early woodcuts to the drawings of artists (like Winslow Homer) that were transferred by craftspeople to wood blocks for mass production.

17. Have students find examples in today's newspapers of drawings of courtroom scenes (where cameras are prohibited) and discuss the problems of artists who make these rapid sketches.

18. Invite one or all of the following to visit your classroom and discuss the processes they work with and the career opportunities in their field:
    - Printer
    - Editorial cartoonist
    - Advertising artist
    - Pasteup artist

19. Take your class to visit a newspaper plant or other printing establishment to learn more about these interrelated jobs that offer visually creative people a chance to use their artistic talents in the modern technological world.[2]

---

[1]**Cross Reference:** Chapter 5, "Sports, Comics, and Other Special Features": VII. Comics; VIII. Discovering the Comics, ACTIVITIES 16–19; IX. Doing Your Own Comics, ACTIVITIES 20–22; X. Comic Strip History, ACTIVITIES 23–28

[2]**Cross Reference:** Chapter 15, "Career Education"

B. PHOTOGRAPHY

The photographer is as vital to the newspaper as the graphic artist and the reporter. As teachers of photography, you can find plenty of examples in the paper for a display.[1] You can follow the suggestions in ACTIVITIES 1 and 2 of this chapter to keep your students aware of photographic events as well as photographers, cinematographers, and video camera people in the news. You can use some of the following activities:

ACTIVITIES

20. Have students clip photos from the newspaper, illustrating photographic techniques as you discuss them.

21. Invite a newspaper photographer to visit the classroom to explain his or her methods and also to discuss career opportunities.

22. Help individual students to arrange to accompany news photographers on their beats.

23. Take your class to visit a newspaper plant to see not only the news photography darkroom, but also other aspects of the printing process that employ photographic technology.[2]

C. PAINTING, SCULPTURE, CRAFTS

For the other visual arts and the crafts, the most effective use of the newspaper (outside of papier-mâché for sculpture and floor protection for painting) is probably the development of a bulletin board similar to the one suggested in Performing Arts, ACTIVITY 1, to keep students constantly aware of events, museum shows, artists, and ideas outside the art room. Arts festivals that bring visual and performing artists together to share achievements, inspire new creation, and discover unsuspected collaborative opportunities are becoming regular summer events throughout the country. Crafts are often included, but craftspeople also have their own even more numerous festivals. Encourage students to attend these whenever possible.

Students are not likely to be asked to review a photography or art exhibition, but they can learn something about the points of critiquing visual art works by reading reviews in the arts pages of the newspaper. If their own works are reviewed, they might consider the suggestions in ACTIVITY 4 in this chapter to achieve a balanced response.

---

[1]**Cross Reference:** Chapter 5, "Sports, Comics, and Other Special Features": XI. Photojournalism; XII. What Makes a Good News Photo? ACTIVITIES 29–34

[2]**Cross Reference:** Chapter 1, "Getting Acquainted with the Newspaper": XI. Producing the Newspaper, ACTIVITY 27

III. SPACE FOR YOUR IDEAS

CHAPTER 11

Social Studies

CONTENTS

Social Studies

The newspaper is, above all, a social studies textbook. Assigning to distinct categories the multitude of social studies activities that can be devised from the newspaper is a task that necessarily results in some overlapping. Although the following ACTIVITIES are grouped as much as possible under appropriate headings, social studies teachers are advised to look through the entire chapter to avoid missing an item that might prove useful.

I. HISTORY

Today's news event is tomorrow's history. Newspaper files are the major sources for history books. One technique that teachers can employ to good advantage is to "teach history backwards." When students read about a current event, ask them to research the background of the event to determine its historical roots. The conflict in the Middle East can be traced back to the creation of the state of Israel in this century, further back to the Crusades, and for more hundreds of years to biblical times. The history of the free press and of its role in the development of democratic society (outlined briefly in Chapter 7, "News and History") is another example. Looking at history backwards helps students to connect the present with the past and to understand why they need to study history.[1]

A. LOOKING BACKWARD

ACTIVITIES

1. Select a current event, and have students trace its roots back through history.

2. Have students create a newspaper for the period in history they are studying.[2] Use a current paper as an example.

3. Compare, from library files, newspapers from earlier times (such as from the Civil War period, World War I, World War II). How do these differ from our papers today? Give students this information during class discussion or assign it as a research project.

---

[1]**Cross Reference:** Chapter 7, "News and History": ACTIVITIES
[2]**Cross Reference:** Chapter 9, "English": ACTIVITIES 27 and 30; Chapter 1: "Getting Acquainted with the Newspaper"; Chapter 2, "What Is News?"

4. Clip any news which parallels American history. Make a file of these articles for use in class discussion. Have students contribute.

5. Have students compare freedom of the press in the United States, Britain, Canada, and other free countries with that in such countries as Russia, Argentina, Cuba, and Poland.

6. Using old files, trace the editorial position of your local daily newspaper on selected major historical issues and ask students to evaluate its success (or failure) in influencing public opinion.

7. Have students trace criticisms of the press through American history and the validity of and motives for the criticisms. The constant battle of presidents (from George Washington onward) with the press is a good one to trace.

B. TECHNOLOGICAL ADVANCES

ACTIVITIES

8. Have students report on humanity's various methods of transportation. Ask them what they can learn about advances made in this area from the newspaper. Have them tell about past methods, present practices, and future plans in your community. Traffic congestion and highway construction are major local issues.

9. Have students identify examples of social and technological changes by comparing historical and contemporary accounts of related events or activities. Ask them to relate contemporary news events to their historical perspective. Examples of issues that have persisted in American history include:

   - Isolationism and foreign involvement
   - The distribution of wealth
   - Race relations
   - Civil liberties
   - Industrialization vs. conservation
   - Relative importance of state and federal rights and powers

10. Have students clip ads, stories, and photos to show that the Industrial Revolution continues today. Include new businesses, industrial developments, and technological advances.

11. Have the class draw generalizations about the causes of labor-management conflicts by analyzing several press-reported strikes. Compare these with strikes in history.

C. MAKING HISTORY

ACTIVITIES

12. Give each student both a copy of a newspaper that is approximately six months old and a copy of today's newspaper. See how many stories they can find in the old paper that are still in the news now. Ask students to select stories from today's paper that they think will still be in the news six months from now. Save the lists, and check the accuracy of the predictions in six months.

13. Have students follow a local or national news story for two weeks, then write up the story as if they were writing for a history book.

14. Have students compile a file of major news stories for two weeks. At the end of that time, ask them to review all the stories and select those they think will appear in history books a hundred years from now. They must give at least one reason for each story they select.

15. Use the daily newspaper to bring up to date your discussions in world history, using articles on such topics as foreign affairs, Common Market, world leaders, discoveries by archeologists, new pacts and treaties, United Nations news, news of countries to be studied.

16. Have students keep a historical calendar on which the most important news of the day is recorded, then mark the most important news of the week. Ask them to keep weekly sheets in a portfolio, recording the news for an entire year. Late in the year, review with students the "important" events to see if they have remained prominent in the news.

17. From your newspaper, obtain wire service copy that did not appear locally. Discuss the reasons why it was excluded. Invite a local newspaper editor to explain how news content is evaluated and selected.[1]

18. Ask students to monitor the evening television news. (A tape recorder will help.) In the next morning's paper, have them mark out the parts of articles included on television. Have them keep a record of TV news, if any, that did not appear in the newspaper. Ask them to evaluate the results.[2]

19. Have students clip articles about the countries you are studying and paste them in a scrapbook with a title such as "Tomorrow's History" or "History in the Making."

---

[1]**Cross Reference:** Chapter 2, "What Is News?": News Values; Chapter 1, "Getting Acquainted with the Newspaper": IX. Comparing Newspapers, ACTIVITIES 17–25

[2]**Cross Reference:** Chapter 8, "The Newspaper Today": ACTIVITIES 2–4

D. HISTORY MAKERS

ACTIVITIES

20. Have students make notebooks containing clippings of news articles in which prominent people are quoted. In each article, ask them to underscore the quote that they think might become famous.

21. Clip all biographical articles on the country's leaders, past and present. Post them, and later file for future reference.

22. Add to the file news and obituary articles about any prominent state, local, national, or international leader who has died.

23. Have students follow the work of famous groups of people around the world—such as the Peace Corps, the United Nations, the Organization of American States, OPEC.

24. Clip reviews of historical books, and post them on the bulletin board. Save them in a file for future reference.

II. GEOGRAPHY

Following the news and actually locating on the map the sites of fast-breaking events will familiarize students with the maps of the world, of their country, of their state and local areas, subjects on which they are, all too often, rather vague. Included at the end of this section are reproducible maps of the world and the United States. These can be useful for some of the map activities that follow.

A. PLACE NAMES AND DATELINES

ACTIVITIES

25. Never pass up an opportunity to study geography. Each time a news story is read, have your students find the location on a map or globe. To reinforce the knowledge, have them record in their notebooks the properly spelled name of the place as well as the country where it is located.

26. Have students scan the datelines of news stories for capital cities of states or counties. Ask them to make a list of the capitals and the country or state of which each is capital.

27. Have students start collecting datelines from each of the fifty United States and post them on the bulletin board. See how long it takes to get all fifty. Keep a count of the

number of times each state appears, and when all fifty states are recorded, compare. Discuss the reasons for the variations.

28. Play the dateline game. Divide the room into teams. One team selects a dateline from a story. The second team is given thirty seconds to locate the area on a map. Award one point for each place correctly located.

B. WHERE IN THE WORLD..?

ACTIVITIES

29. Divide a bulletin board into sections and have students place news clippings under the headings: local, state, national, and international. Appoint students to be responsible for changing the clippings each day.

30. Using a large map of the world, connect a news item from the paper to the spot where the news was made with a piece of string or yarn.

31. Have students keep in their notebooks a map of the world. When the news of any country is reported, have them place the name of the country on the map and color it. Students should share their news to help the whole class complete their maps.

32. Have students clip maps from the paper which show territorial changes caused by treaties, reorganizations of government, wars, or new nations having won their independence. Discuss these in class before mounting for placement in notebooks or on the bulletin board.

33. Using a map of the world, help students to designate the countries belonging to NATO, SEATO, OAS, the Warsaw Pact, OPEC. Have them clip articles concerning nations belonging to these organizations and articles about the organizations themselves. These can be used for a bulletin board display.

34. Have students find a news story that gives some background information about one of the United States. See how many states they can find mentioned in the newspaper, and have the class work together to develop an encyclopedia of states.

C. YOUR OWN COMMUNITY

ACTIVITIES

35. Have students collect pictures, news items, and advertisements to illustrate the many recreational facilities found in your city, county, or state. These can be presented as reports or used to make notebooks or bulletin board displays.

36. Have students collect news stories about specific kinds of happenings in your town and in surrounding towns. On a bulletin board with a map of your local area, post the articles and connect them to their point of origin with string or yarn.

37. Using the advertisements in the paper, have students illustrate the types of business and industry to be found in your community. Ask what geographical features caused them to locate there.

38. Have students locate by latitude and longitude the cities from which major sports events are reported.

39. Have students interpret maps and diagrams of land formations. (See pages 193–194.)

III. GOVERNMENT/POLITICAL SCIENCE

ACTIVITIES in this section cover the role of the press in a free society, the Bill of Rights and Constitution, functions of government, the electoral process, taxes,* local government, special-interest conflicts, foreign affairs, political leaders, and good citizenship.

A. THE FREE PRESS

ACTIVITIES

40. To help students discover how the First Amendment works to guarantee the public's right to free speech and access to information through the press, have them do the following:

Divide into groups of three. Each group chooses a special interest to represent, such as top government officials (local, state, or national); welfare recipients; minority groups; anti-abortion groups; union executives/members; U.S. president and White House staff; a foreign nation; political terrorists; anti-nuclear protestors; conscientious objectors; professional organizations (medicine, education, journalism, law, etc.); environmental protection groups. Best choices are those currently in the news. Each special interest group **censors** one day's paper, cutting out all articles, photos,

*Cross Reference: V. Economics

Name _____ Date _____

MAP 1—UNITED STATES

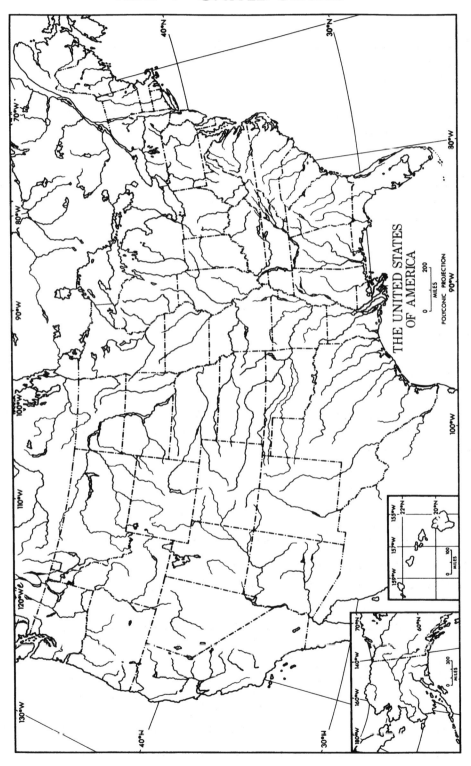

Name _____ Date _____

MAP 2—THE WORLD

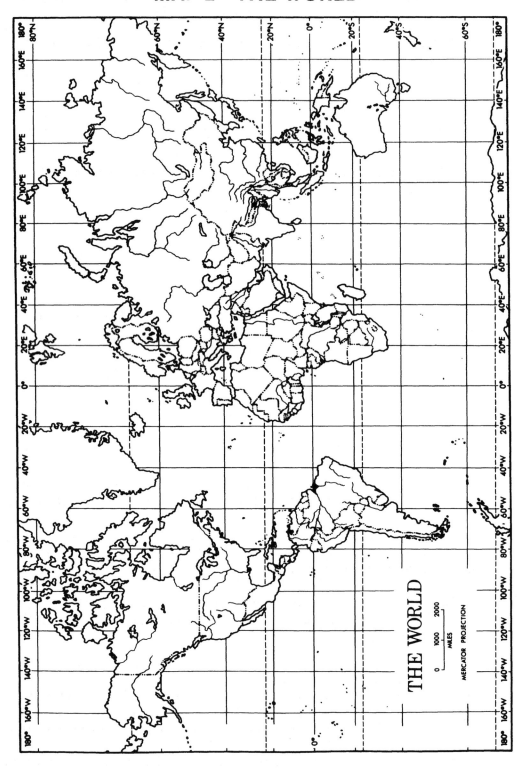

editorials, headlines, display ads, classified ads, and comics which might disagree with any of their beliefs and pastes them on a poster board for display. Class discussion following this exercise should ask:

- What reasons does your group have for censoring the material you cut out? Would you like to maintain this right to censor?

- What problems do you see in allowing a group to censor the newspaper?

- What about the mistakes a newspaper makes? Can they be prevented?

- Are there fair ways to allow individuals or groups to control what a newspaper reports?

- What avenues are open to groups who feel they are not getting enough (or the right kind of) newspaper publicity?

- Should a newspaper ever be restrained from publishing facts or opinions?

- Whom does freedom of the press benefit?

Have the class research (individually or in groups) and report on any current legal restrictions on freedom of the press.[1]

41. Have a class discussion, considering the extent to which the press should function as a watchdog of government.

42. Have students evaluate the reliability of articles by judging the source. For example: "the president said," "the White House announced," "an informed spokesman said," "all Washington believes," etc. Why are these vague attributions used?

43. Have the class debate the advantages and disadvantages of an "advocacy" press in contemporary America.

44. Have students clip and paste in a notebook, or for display, comic strips which keep up with current affairs. Ask them to point out the event or story with which they deal.

45. Have students prepare reports on a current civic, state, or national problem using editorials from several papers, cartoons, and opinions of political leaders. Compare these with the opinions expressed by the public in letters to the editor.

46. Define **conservative, moderate, liberal**. Have students group your newspaper's editorial writers and syndicated columnists into the three groups. Are all sides represented in your newspaper?[2]

[1]**Cross Reference:** Chapter 8, "The Newspaper Today": II. Responsibility and Freedom and following sections. Adapted from *The Newspaper as an Effective Teaching Tool*, Washington, D.C., the American Newspaper Publishers Association Foundation, 1977, with their permission.

[2]**Cross Reference:** Chapter 1, "Getting Acquainted with the Newspaper": X. Criteria for a Good Newspaper

47. Have students write a letter to the editor that is constructively critical of the editorial position of the newspaper on some given issue.*

B. THE CONSTITUTION

ACTIVITIES

48. Using the Bill of Rights as background, have students list the freedoms and rights found there and try to find news articles that defend these rights, are dependent on these rights, or even mention these rights. Compile information into a report that demonstrates that the Bill of Rights is very much alive today. Devote special attention to the ERA (Equal Rights Amendment), and conduct a debate over whether it is a necessary addition to the Bill of Rights.

49. Have students collect in a notebook all articles relating to the United States Constitution (such as Supreme Court rulings, proposed amendments, cases from other courts that involve questions of constitutional rights).

50. To show how the system of checks and balances works, have students collect articles about the activities of the three branches of government: legislative, executive, and judicial.

Many political scientists feel that, in recent decades, the executive branch of the federal government has come to dominate the legislative branch. In ACTIVITY 51, students review the historical problems Congress has faced in counterbalancing presidential power. It will succeed if students come away convinced that the abstract term "checks and balances" relates directly to the candidates they will vote for some day, to the government services they enjoy, to the government controls they are subjected to, and to the watchdog role of their free press.

51. Assign groups of students to analyze shifts in legislative and executive power since the Civil War (a group for each major period). Have the class document these shifts and chart the reasons for them on the chalkboard or in a notebook. Over a period of several months, have the class devise a method for clipping from the daily paper articles which deal with the conflict between today's legislative and executive leaders. At the end of this time, have them analyze the clippings and develop a final document identifying trends in the balance of power. In the process, have them consider the following questions:

    – Do you think the framers of the Constitution realized that the checks and balances they wrote in would cause friction and delay in running the government? Why didn't they develop a system which works more efficiently?

*Cross Reference: Chapter 4, "The Editorial Pages": VII. Letters to the Editor

- What historically have been the major sources of conflict between the executive and legislative branches? Are there conflicts which once existed that no longer matter? Are there entirely new conflicts today?

- What procedures and regulations in Congress have kept the House and Senate from acting swiftly and showing more leadership?

- What effect does the period between elections have on the relative power of Congress?

- What opportunities does the president have to exercise power that the legislative branch lacks?

- How does the free press function to check and balance both president and Congress? Is this function in the Constitution too?

Conclusion: Students write their individual opinions on what will happen to the balance of power between the executive and legislative branches in the next ten years.*

C. CONGRESS

ACTIVITIES

52. Have students clip from the paper the proceedings of Congress. With this information, ask them to plan a debate as it might have happened in that body.

53. Watch for the reporting of new bills passed by Congress and signed by your congressional representative. Post these on the bulletin board and call them to the attention of the class.

54. Have students keep up on new bills and amendments passed at both federal and state levels. Have them label the articles and write brief summaries, to be posted on the bulletin board.

55. Have students collect articles that tell of the work of some of the committees of Congress (such as agriculture, foreign affairs, banking and finance). These may be used as the basis of a list summarizing the services offered by the government.

56. Have students read a report of a meeting of your state, city, or national legislature. Have a group plan a presentation of this information to the class as they think it might have happened.

*Adapted from *The Newspaper as an Effective Teaching Tool*, Washington, D.C., the American Newspaper Publishers Association Foundation, 1977, with their permission.

57. Have students collect articles illustrating the functions of the various levels and branches of government for use in studying the power and duties of regulatory agencies.

D. GOVERNMENT CONTROL

ACTIVITIES

58. Have students collect articles about the various regulatory agencies (such as the Federal Trade Commission, Federal Communications Commission, Interstate Commerce Commission) and other types of agencies that affect business (such as the Federal Reserve, the stock market, the Farm Bureau).

59. Have students predict the response of a government official or agency to a current news event.

60. Have students collect articles that demonstrate government control or backing of business and industry. Plan a debate on the topic: "Government control is too much" (or not enough).

E. TAXES

ACTIVITIES

61. Have students collect articles, pictures, and ads that illustrate all the ways we pay taxes (including sales tax, gasoline tax, alcohol tax, tobacco tax, income tax, property tax).

62. Have students make a poster labeling each type of tax and add to their vocabulary notebook other items about taxes, underlining such terms as real estate tax, surtax, excise tax, appraisal, direct tax, withholding tax. They should learn the meaning of each word they underline.

63. In a class discussion, have students evaluate the advantages and disadvantages of various types of taxes described in news articles, features, editorials, and analytical columns.

64. Have students choose any controversial issue and clip everything they can find about it over a period of time. Organize a panel discussion presenting the opinions of various people.

F. ELECTIONS

ACTIVITIES

65. Follow the news of a political campaign. Have students clip news articles about candidates, reports of speeches, campaign releases. From this collection, they are to outline the platform of each candidate and to compare the platforms in a class discussion.

66. Have students compare the platforms and policies of two competing candidates by analyzing their reported statements.

67. Have students conduct a class or school mock election after analysis of the issues reported during the campaign.

G. PUBLIC LEADERS

ACTIVITIES

68. Collect articles and photos about famous leaders in the world. Create a *Hall of Fame* or a *Who's Who* for the classroom library.

69. Have students work in pairs and develop an imaginary interview, with one playing the role of reporter and the other, that of an important public figure. Base questions and answers on recent news.*

70. Clip stories about people who have been doing good things for the community. At the end of every week, have students choose one to receive the Good Citizen's Award for the week.

71. Government officials and political figures are often caricatured in political cartoons. Have students collect as many as possible and match them with real photos from the newspaper. Discuss the accuracy and fairness of the cartoons.

---

*Cross Reference: Chapter 3, "Features: The Other Kind of News": IV. Steps for a Successful Interview (R)

H. LOCAL GOVERNMENT

ACTIVITIES

72. Have students read about problems in your community, then write an essay or speech, beginning with "If I were Mayor...," stating a problem and what they would do about it.

73. Compare local needs, as perceived by students, with the local budget, as reported in the newspaper.

74. Have students attend a meeting of your city council or a comparable body. Have them write a news article afterward and compare it with the newspaper account.

75. Plan a visit to a meeting of the Board of Selectmen or the State Legislature. Watch for the newspaper account of the meeting. Discuss the accuracy of the news report.

76. Follow major decisions of the Board of Education in news reports. Have students attempt to establish a rationale for the decisions.

77. Have students draw an editorial cartoon related to a current local issue.

I. WORLDWIDE

ACTIVITIES

78. Use newspaper stories as the basis for grouping foreign countries into those friendly and those unfriendly to the United States. Have students mark specific statements to support their decisions.

79. Have students clip news stories to make a chart of protest techniques around the world and have them indicate which ones are effective, which ones ineffective.

IV. SOCIOLOGY/ANTHROPOLOGY

Are crime and law enforcement matters of political science or sociology? Both, undoubtedly. Here you will find reference to them under sociology, along with community and interpersonal relations, customs and cultural values, and the problems of minorities, including teenagers.

A. CRIME AND PUNISHMENT

ACTIVITIES

80. This small group project will help students make objective judgments about the role of the police in their community. Over a three-week period, have them collect all available information about police in their community (news coverage as well as public information material from the local government). They should also interview ten people in the community, asking some of the following questions:

    - Have you ever had to call the police for help?

    - How did they respond? Did you get the help you needed?

    - Do you feel that the police are really "on the job," protecting you, your home, your community, and the people in it?

    - What do you recall hearing or reading about the police force in recent weeks?

Group members should also interview several members of the police force to find out more about them, their jobs, and how they feel about their work and the community. Possible questions:

    - What are your regular duties?

    - What unusual incidents have happened to you in carrying out your duties? Did they involve personal danger? How did you feel at the time?

    - Is your salary adequate compensation for what you do?

    - How do you feel about this community? About the various groups in it? What do you think they feel about you?

    - What do you think of newspaper coverage of police work?

The group presents its findings to the class in the method of its choice—charts, collages, debates, panel discussions, visits by police representatives, reports, role-playing demonstrations. Several class sessions should be scheduled. This topic, of great interest and controversy among young people, is capable of stimulating strong class interaction.

Analysis questions for students to consider:

    - What, according to your findings, are the duties of the police in your community? In your estimation, which duties are more important?

    - What general attitudes do you find among citizens toward the police, and vice versa?

    - What risks must the police take in protecting the community?

    - Are the police engaged in efforts to better police-community relations, especially with young people?

    - Do you believe there are other attempts that could be made to help citizens, especially young people, and the police to work together?

    - What part can the newspaper play in insuring effective police protection? Does your newspaper give enough coverage of police activities?

To evaluate results of this project, members of the small group develop a questionnaire on knowledge about and attitudes toward the police to be given to class members before and after the class presentation. Shifts in responses are graphed. Each group member writes a subjective essay describing any changes in his or her views about the functioning and performance of police in society as a result of this study.[1]

81. From published information about selected persons convicted of representative crimes, have students estimate the social class of the convicts and correlate with the sentences they receive.

82. Set up a courtroom in your class. "Try" a case from details listed in a news article about a crime. In selecting the article, have the class discuss whether the testimony reported before the verdict is reached in any way constitutes "trial by newspaper."[2]

B. THE NEWSPAPER MIRRORS CULTURE

ACTIVITIES

83. Discuss the social and economic consequences if there were no newspapers.

84. Have students develop a profile of local beliefs and values by following local news, editorials, and ads.

85. Have students clip articles and pictures as evidence of the culture of your community. Include notices of art exhibits, musical events, advances in education, lectures by prominent people. Use the material to create an attractive collage or poster.

86. An alternate individual project would be to make a booklet to send to a pen pal or someone in a foreign country which includes pictures and advertisements of parks, recreational facilities, businesses, educational facilities, transportation, types of homes, etc., in your community and area.

87. Have students compose a social customs booklet for a space traveler who lands on earth. Collect newspaper clippings of weddings, parades, festivals, awards, and everyday gestures.

88. Collect pictures of the art, musical festivals, costumes, or anything which shows the culture of other nations of the world. File these for use as bulletin boards or posters during your discussion of that country.

---

[1] Adapted from *The Newspaper as an Effective Teaching Tool*, Washington, D.C., the American Newspaper Publishers Association Foundation, 1977, with their permission.

[2] **Cross Reference:** Chapter 8, "The Newspaper Today": IV. Fair Trial

89. Have students collect examples from the newspaper that illustrate the effect of society on the environment. Include stories and pictures of dams, irrigation systems, mining, forestry, and industrial development.

90. Help students identify American social values implied by selected display advertisements.

91. Have students categorize the amusement interests of American society as inferred from movie and television ads and movies. Discuss the implications of these interests.

92. Ask students to identify the contemporary social values reflected in selected comic strips.

93. Compare class or school responses in opinion polls to national poll results on the same questions as reported in the press.

94. From published public records, have students compare marriage and divorce rates in your area with national rates. Discuss the implications of the comparison.

95. Have students classify the social philosophies of authors of letters to the editor over an extended period.

96. Have students collect the work of an editorial cartoonist over an extended period and describe his or her philosophy through examination of the cartoons.

97. Have students read newspapers from three different areas. Discuss the prominence and extent of coverage of a particular event or subject. Have them infer how this reflects the diversification of interests in our society.

C. RACIAL ISSUES

ACTIVITIES

98. Have students categorize the issue in a reported racial conflict. For example: economic problems, legal rights, education, dignity, etc.

99. Remind students that, in categorizing (classifying), they may be stereotyping. Have them collect cartoons that represent different stereotypes (such as teenager, politician, rotten kid, senior citizen, lawman). Discuss why stereotyping is usually inaccurate.*

100. Identify examples of ethnocentrism in newspaper accounts of life in various geographic situations.

*Cross Reference: Chapter 9, "English": II. Language, A. Semantics

D. THE GENERATION GAP

ACTIVITIES

101. Have students find all the stories in today's paper which are about young people. Are these good news stories or bad news stories? How does this affect public opinion about young people?

102. Identify the beliefs, attitudes, and values that constitute the so-called generation gap by keeping a file of articles showing the views of younger and older people. Discuss with students the validity of the reports on younger people.

103. As an individual project, have a student prepare a booklet of newspaper articles, syndicated columns, and photos for a young couple planning a family. Topics should include prenatal care, care of small children, marital problems, and accidents in the home.

104. Have students collect news articles that show people's tendency to join a group and to interact between groups. Examples could include Boy and Girl Scouts, 4-H, sports teams, etc. Examine the interdependence of these groups.

105. From newspaper accounts, ask students to identify a community problem that can be solved by teenagers. Take appropriate social action.

E. MISCELLANEOUS

ACTIVITIES

106. In a class discussion, compare explanations of cause and effect in news articles with appropriate social science generalizations about human behavior.

107. Have students find an article about a crisis situation. Have them develop an analysis of the problem: Who is involved? What were the causes? What are the possible outcomes?

108. Have students develop a classification system for traffic fatalities (time of day, one or more cars, age and sex of driver, alcohol-related, etc.) and chart them for an extended period. Based on the data compiled, discuss possible ways to reduce fatalities.

V. ECONOMICS

When you include advertising, there is no question that the newspaper contains more information on economics than on any other subject. The following ACTIVITIES cover business conditions, finance, taxation, foreign trade, labor, agriculture, housing, advertising, and transportation.*

A. TRENDS, SUPPLY, AND DEMAND

ACTIVITIES

109. Have students spend some time getting acquainted with the financial pages of the daily newspaper. Ask them to make a list of any unfamiliar terminology and to check its meaning in the dictionary. The list should be added to regularly.

110. Keep a clipping file on current economic topics, and ask students to make regular contributions. Every few weeks compare articles on related topics in a discussion of trends.

111. Have students scan newspapers for charts and graphs related to population changes, employment, production, price and wage changes, and other phases of national economics. Spend some time helping them learn to interpret the data correctly.

112. Compare columns and analytical articles by authorities in the field on a given economic topic. Ask students which ones are more convincing and have them explain why.

113. Watch business activity in the newspaper, particularly the stock market. Point out to students that, if business is poor for the car salespeople, for example, they will notice an almost instant rise in the amount of newspaper space devoted to car ads. When they read stories about the high prices of food items, pork, for instance, they will see fewer ads for bacon and more, perhaps, for hamburger.

114. Try the following project to help students learn some of the effects of shortages of resources or products. Over a period of a month or two, have them collect a class clipping file on any newspaper coverage of resources or products in short supply locally, nationally, or internationally. Tell them to extend their search to editorials, ads, business and stock market reporting, and other types of information that reflect shortages in supply. The scarce item may be of minor significance (Cabbage Patch dolls, for example) or vital (oil, for example). Once the file is well stocked, let the class divide itself in any way it determines in order to:

    – Categorize the resources or products in short supply

    – Analyze and chart the difficulties each shortage is causing

---

*For ACTIVITIES pertaining to economics and management at the household level, see Chapter 14, "Consumer Education."

Questions to consider in analysis:

- How does this shortage affect you personally?

- Has the shortage affected prices of this and other products?

- How does it affect business in general? Which specific businesses or industries are particularly affected?

- Is this a crucial product? In other words, could you get along without it or use substitutes?

- What are governments, businesses, and private individuals doing about this shortage? Could they be doing more? What, in general, is the public reaction to the situation?

- Why is this resource or product in short supply? Can you find specific proof that the shortage is as real and crucial as it seems?

Have students brainstorm together to develop some general statements they can make after their research about the cause-and-effect relationship between supply and demand. Compare these with the basic supply and demand theories (explained in a good economics textbook).*

115. It is possible to analyze business conditions somewhat roughly on the basis of the number and type of classified ads in the newspaper. Have your class check help wanted ads, apartments for rent, houses for sale. If you can secure back issues of the paper, make comparisons. Have students develop charts on the basis of what they discover and estimate the economic health of the community according to these tabulations.

116. If your paper publishes a year-end section on business conditions and business prospects, have students spend some time studying this and make some predictions about what the future may have in store.

117. Have students hunt in the newspaper for statements by government officials and other economists about present and future business conditions. Are what these people are saying facts or opinions? Do the opinions seem to be unbiased, or is there usually special motivation for what is said?

118. Assign the class the topic "The Industrial Revolution Continues." Ask them to put in their notebooks or on the bulletin board articles that show the factory system and mass production are still evolving. What are some of the sweeping changes in technology?

119. Have students shop for their dream house in the real estate ads. Have them note the price of houses in your community. Explain how the real estate market affects the economy of the area.

*Adapted from *The Newspaper as an Effective Teaching Tool*, Washington, D.C., the American Newspaper Publishers Association Foundation, 1977, with their permission.

B. ADVERTISING

ACTIVITIES

120. Discuss the fact that the newspaper costs nearly $1.00 per copy to produce yet the newsstand price is less. Why? (*Answer:* Advertising revenue.)*

121. Have students use the advertising in the daily paper to determine the types of businesses and industry located in the community.

122. Have students find examples of national advertising, local retail advertising, and classified advertising for a bulletin board display. Use this as the basis of a class discussion on the place of advertising in our national economy.

123. In a class discussion, list the services in your community that would be difficult or impossible to carry out without the help of advertising. Have students locate newspaper ads to illustrate each point.

124. Study advertisements in the newspaper to learn the five fundamentals of good advertising:

   – Get attention through positive treatment
   – Show people advantages of the product
   – Create a need for the product
   – Persuade people to buy the product
   – Ask for action from the buyer

   Ask students to find ads in the newspaper that meet these standards and demonstrate each point.

125. Have students devise ads to sell a product during the "high price or scarcity times" and for the same product during "overproduction times." (See ACTIVITY 114, page 205.)

C. GOVERNMENT CONTROL

ACTIVITIES

126. Clip newspaper articles that illustrate the government's role in business: setting standards for weights and measurements, providing inspection and licensing, arbitrating disputes, etc. Compile a file for use in class discussion.

127. Have students make a special section in their notebooks for articles on the activities of such organizations as the Federal Trade Commission, the Federal Reserve, the Interstate Commerce Commission, the Farm Bureau, etc.

---

*Cross Reference: Chapter 6, "Advertising: More Than Half the Paper"

D. THE STOCK MARKET

ACTIVITIES

128. Have your classes study the rise and fall of the stock market generally for a period of time. Use the Dow Jones averages or some similar means of comparison. Discuss reasons given in newspapers for rises and falls and consider also students' theories explaining market fluctuations. Let students role-play as market analysts. Draw attention to the weekly public television show, "Wall $treet Week" with financial journalist Louis Rukeyser.

129. Invite a local broker to talk to the class. Have students prepare for his or her visit by compiling a list of questions from their reading of the financial pages.

130. Organize a classroom broker's office and have students "buy" and "sell" stocks for a period of time, basing their decisions on information obtained from the newspaper. Commissions should be added to all purchase prices and subtracted from selling prices.

131. Have students make graphs showing the rise and fall of at least three stocks, following them in the newspaper for a period of several weeks.

132. Have each student "invest" $1,000 in one stock (or several), follow its rise and fall in the newspaper, and graph the fluctuations. Have students make posters which include these graphs and clippings of stock quotations from the newspaper.

133. Collect brochures from banks, savings and loan associations, and similar organizations concerning making loans and accepting deposits. Have the class compare all these for rates of interest for saving and borrowing.

134. From newspaper reports, have students compute for various companies ratios of earnings to sales, both before and after allowance for taxes. Also compute dividend rates in relation to market prices.

E. THE NATIONAL DEBT

ACTIVITY

135. Collect current newspaper articles and information on issues pertaining to the national debt. Organize the class into committees to study the pro and con of each of these expenditures for: national defense, foreign aid, social welfare programs, etc. Conduct a panel discussion in which each committee presents its reasons for continuing national spending in its area. Let the rest of the class be the opposition.

F. FOREIGN AID

ACTIVITY

136. Use articles collected by students on U.S. aid to foreign countries for a study of the problems involved. Have the class decide what criteria ought to be met by countries receiving help. Build a file of newspaper clippings for reference.

G. TAXATION

ACTIVITIES

137. Have students define the different types of taxes they find reference to in the newspaper. (See also III. Government/Political Science, D. Government Control, ACTIVITIES 59 and 60, page 198.)

138. Have students prepare a notebook of tax articles.

139. Using the newspaper as an information source, have students react to a proposed tax. Have them work in pairs, take opposing views, and debate the issue before the class.

140. Have students study the newspaper for articles on tax-related matters—federal, state, and local. Have them consider their trip to school that morning and make a list of everything connected with the trip for which citizens pay taxes. Have them make some generalizations about the necessities of taxes. Ask them if their feelings about taxes have changed.

141. Have students gather information from the newspaper for a debate on either or both of these topics.

    - Resolved: that churches and other religious and charitable institutions should pay local property taxes.
    - Resolved: that municipally-owned utilities should be subject to property and income taxation.

H. BANKRUPTCY

ACTIVITY

142. In the field of business bankruptcy, have students study newspaper files on a major bankruptcy case such as the *Pennsylvania Railroad* (1968) or *Braniff Airlines* (1983). What caused the collapse? What help did the government give and what further help, if any, do they think the government should provide under such circumstances?

I. LABOR

ACTIVITIES

143. Have students read a newspaper feature on a job action dispute. Follow the news to see if a strike develops. Is money the main issue?

144. Make a study of a strike involving public servants such as teachers, firefighters, sanitation workers. Divide the class into labor, management, the public, and federal mediators. Have each group collect information from the newspaper to make a case for their position. After several days of preparation, devote a class period to hearings, negotiations, and a resolution of the strike. If it is settled before the end of the school year, compare students' solutions to what really happened.

145. Have students find an example in the paper of an occupational group that wants more pay (farmers, miners, etc.). Find out why they have the problem. Has it been solved?

146. Have students study the newspaper for several weeks before writing a paper entitled "Do Labor Unions Have Too Much Power?" They may take either side.

147. Ask students to find evidence in the newspaper that a machine has replaced a large number of people. Ask them to write a short report on how this affects the economy.

148. Have students make a study of the Social Security system, based on the many analytical articles, columns, and debates in Congress reported in the newspaper. Have them try to decide whether it is fair, what it costs the taxpayer, and whether it works.

149. Have the class follow trends in national unemployment in the newspaper, locate the areas of unemployment, and try to discover the causes and effects.

J. FACTORS OF PRODUCTION

ACTIVITY

150. A major project to help students understand the four basic factors of production—land, labor, capital, and management—can be organized as follows.

Divide the class into three groups, representing small non-plant business; medium-size plant business; large factory business. Each group must make the following analyses:

- *Land:* Turn to the classified section of your newspaper, and look for business space to rent. From the kind of business you are running, decide what type of "land" you require. Keeping good records, decide how much the space will cost you per month and year.

- *Labor:* Again in the classified ad section, look at Help Wanted ads for the type of labor you require. See if the salary for this type of job is listed, and figure this amount into your budget. Follow the same procedure for additional labor.

- *Capital:* Look at the bank ads and the business section and figure how much initial capital you will need, how much working capital. Don't forget to consider the cost of utilities and other operating expenses. Your plan should include paying off all loans, principal and interest, within a three-year period. Keep good records of all your transactions.

- *Management:* Prepare an organizational chart or chain of command for your business to decide which type of business management you want to have. With the help of the classified ad section, start with your clerical help and laborers. Determine what duties they will perform and to whom each worker will report. Move up the line, determining who has authority over whom and where each person falls in the organizational chart.

Each business should prepare some kind of display and be able to explain its operation to the rest of the class.

VI. SPACE FOR YOUR IDEAS

CHAPTER 12

Science

CONTENTS

Science

Students are probably more aware of science in the news than of most of their other school subjects. Teachers can further sharpen their awareness by bringing into class discussion newspaper articles particularly pertinent to the topic under study. Better still, have students bring them in. A few ACTIVITIES for any science class are listed here, followed by those relating to specific areas.

GENERAL

ACTIVITIES

1. Have students organize themselves to plan and keep up to date a bulletin board of news clippings concerning your subject and related information and events. Focus on one of these clippings for a brief class discussion at least once a week, more often if possible.

2. Several times a semester, have students work in groups to develop oral or illustrated presentations on topics related to your study that have been prominent in the news.

3. Have students search the help wanted sections of the newspaper for jobs requiring some knowledge of science. Discuss jobs that have changed or been affected by scientific advancements.

4. Jobs found in ACTIVITY 3 should be listed by categories and the number of jobs in each category charted for bulletin board display over a period of several months. At the end of this time, have students study this chart to prepare for class discussion, a quiz, or a written report on what seem to be the best job opportunities in science-related fields.*

5. Have students add to the classroom bulletin board a Who's Who section of scientists in the news. Have individual students present brief reports on these people from time to time. The rest of the class is required to ask questions and engage in discussions concerning the importance, values, and possible disadvantages of the work each scientist is doing.

6. After students have become familiar with a number of scientific personalities and their achievements, play a "Who Am I?" game. Pin articles about them on students' backs

---

*Cross Reference: Chapter 15, "Career Education"

and have them try to guess who they are by asking their classmates questions. This can be done at several levels of sophistication.

7. As students read science-related articles, have them keep a vocabulary notebook of unfamiliar words. They may find newly created words that are not in the classroom dictionary.

8. Ask students to find as many examples as they can of the use of the metric system in the newspaper. Have them interview ten people on their feelings about converting to the metric system. Report the findings to the class.*

9. Have students find mention in the newspaper of as many agencies of the national, state, and local government as they can that use scientific data in setting regulations, etc. Have them decide in which areas of science workers for these agencies must be trained. Have them evaluate the scientific credibility of the spokespeople for these agencies quoted in the newspaper.

I. BIOLOGY

A. PLANTS, ANIMALS, ECOLOGY, AGRICULTURE

ACTIVITIES

10. Select a pastoral photograph from a newspaper. Have students list all the flora and fauna they would expect to find in this setting.

11. Locate articles about the uses of the forests in your state. Ask students how forests are repopulated. How many products can they name that come from the forests?

12. Start a class ecology bulletin board. Post newspaper photos and stories on ecology problems. Ask students to add to it daily.

13. Have students look for articles on plant life, animal life, marine life, genetic discoveries, cell structure, etc. for a clipping file. Discuss the most exciting ones as soon as they are brought in. Save others to pull out when they become pertinent to current course work.

14. Place on the bulletin board and bring into discussion frequently articles about the food chain, world food supplies, new methods of agriculture, organic agriculture, etc.

*Cross Reference: Chapter 13, "Math": III. Weights and Measures

15. Have students study the commodities futures on the financial page for discussion of the relationship of agriculture/plant life to economics.

B. HEALTH AND SAFETY

ACTIVITIES

16. Ask students to separate the items in a food store ad into the four basic food groups. Develop a balanced meal from items in the ads.

17. Search the newspaper ads to see if any foods provide a list of ingredients. Ask students why they think the company decided to supply or omit the list.

18. Determine the calorie content of foods your students eat frequently. Using newspaper ads, compare the cost and value of these foods.

19. Have your students collect various diets listed in the newpaper. Plan a healthful menu for five days.

20. Have students keep a running list of items mentioned in the newspaper that are hazardous to human health. Post the list on the bulletin board.

21. Have students find a newspaper ad for cigarettes. Have them list the methods used by the advertiser to convince the reader that smoking is a good thing to do.

22. Use newspaper ads and articles about tobacco smoking. Ask students to find the differences between science/health articles and the ads. Which are more convincing?

23. Have students find newspaper articles on alcohol and drug abuse. What problems are presented and what solutions offered? Have students prepare a panel discussion.

24. Have students find ads and news stories about items which could be dangerous to small children and/or adults. Have them develop a set of safety rules for using the items selected.

25. Construct safety posters for the use of power tools using newspaper articles and pictures.*

26. Keep a list of all accidents reported in the newspaper for a period of one week. Ask students to make generalizations from this information. What type of accident was

*Cross Reference: Chapter 14, "Consumer Education": IV Home Management, D. Home Building and Maintenance

most frequently reported? What accidents caused the most bodily injury? The least? What are some precautions that could have prevented these accidents?

27. Ask students to make posters from newspaper pictures and articles on the following: toy safety, meals for the elderly, bicycle safety.

28. Ask students to search newspapers for items which are useful when used correctly but could be dangerous when misused or used by young children. Examples: knives, mowers, power tools, disinfectants. Discuss safeguards for each.

29. Have students find the number of electrical appliances mentioned in today's paper. Ask them to consider how the increased use of such appliances could overload circuits in older houses. Discuss the results and methods of prevention.

C. PHYSICAL EDUCATION

ACTIVITIES

30. Ask your students to review the sports pages. Have them list the advantages of each sport in a physical fitness program.

31. Have students collect articles on exercise from the newspaper and work in groups to plan a program of exercise for one class session.

D. MEDICINE

ACTIVITIES

32. Have students collect newspaper articles that tell of advances in medicine. Ask students to predict what diseases will be conquered in the next ten years, based on evidence in the articles.

33. Have students read the medical columns in the newspaper and list the medical problems discussed. What ailments are mentioned most often? What diseases are the leading cause of death in the country? What preventive measures are currently most recommended?

34. Hold a class debate on the subject: "Should medical doctors be allowed to advertise their services in the newspaper?"

35. Ask students to collect ads for over-the-counter medicines. Have them discuss the accuracy of the claims made by these ads.

36. Have students follow the activities of major health organizations as reported in the newspaper. They should look for the following:

    - American Medical Association
    - American Heart Association
    - American Dental Association
    - American Cancer Society
    - American Red Cross
    - Others

E. MENTAL HEALTH

ACTIVITIES

37. Have students search the newspaper for all the mental health services that are available in your area. Have them determine the cost of these services. Do the same for other health services.

38. Select from the newspaper pictures which show various emotions. Discuss the way people handle their emotions. Do the stories with these pictures confirm the students' suggestions?

39. Comic strips offer a study in personality conflicts. These can be examined by students using values clarification techniques.

40. Follow a murder investigation in the newspaper where the accused is pleading innocent by reason of insanity. Discuss with the class the origin of this plea and the growing controversy about its validity as reported in the newspaper.

II. CHEMISTRY

ACTIVITIES

41. Clip photographs or drawings of articles that are made by people and other articles that are not. Have students place each photograph in its proper category.

42. Categorize pictures of products and advertisements for products into natural and synthetic classifications. Ask students to research how some of the synthetic products are made.

43. Have students research how paper is made. When they have completed the research, have them soak some newsprint in water to break down the fibers that compose it. The ink used on newspapers is oil based and will float to the top of the water.

44. Have students find newspaper articles about the disposal of solid or liquid wastes. Have them discover what chemical processes are used.

III. ENVIRONMENT

A. WEATHER

ACTIVITIES

45. Follow the weather forecast for several days. Have students make a line graph of high and low temperatures.

46. Follow the published weather report for a given location for an extended period and account for it by applying meteorological theories.

47. Record weather predictions and actual weather conditions for a period of two weeks. How accurate were the predictions? Ask students to speculate why some of the predictions were wrong.

48. Collect the weather maps from the newspaper for several days or weeks. Ask students to place them in the correct sequence and then to make generalizations about how weather systems tend to move.

49. Trace the progress of a major storm on the weather map.

50. Have students use the weather map to predict tomorrow's weather. Record student predictions and compare with the actual weather the next day.

51. Ask students to locate ten articles over a period of time about natural or weather phenomena such as earthquakes, tornadoes, hurricanes, and major storms. Complete the project by having the class write a research report on one of the phenomena.

52. Discuss why so-called "natural disasters" such as those reported in the articles for ACTIVITY 51 occur and suggest ways to alleviate the risks.

B. HUMAN IMPACT ON THE ENVIRONMENT

ACTIVITIES

53. Ask students to find articles that show a natural resource being used. Is it being used wisely?

54. Collect stories that show human impact on the environment. Use these as a basis for class discussion.

55. Have students make a collage of newspaper pictures to illustrate threats to our environment, such as acid rain, soil erosion, toxic waste disposal, strip mining, offshore oil drilling, etc.

56. Have students locate current examples of how human beings have modified their geographic environment.

57. Have students project the environmental impact of a new factory, highway, housing development, or other construction project under discussion in their community.

IV. PHYSICS

A. MECHANICS

ACTIVITIES

58. Have students collect as many pictures and drawings as possible from the newspaper that show simple machines.

59. Have students search the comics for situations which defy the laws of science. Have them explain, using these laws, why the situation is impossible.

B. ENERGY

ACTIVITIES

60. Clip articles and photographs for an energy notebook. What are our energy problems? What resources do we have? What forms of energy will we be using in fifty years?

61. Have students make a collage of newspaper pictures illustrating energy conservation, such as solar, hydro power, wind power, and more efficient combustion.

62. Ask students to find all advertisements in today's newspaper which claim to save energy. How much energy would be saved if all these things were done? Have the class analyze the claims and decide which ones seem accurate, which exaggerated.

63. Have students collect articles about hearings and discussions surrounding the construction of nuclear power plants. List all facts mentioned both for and against. Discuss these in class.

64. Look for articles about breeder reactors. Use a physics book to research the dangers involved.

V. ASTRONOMY AND SPACE

ACTIVITIES

65. Use the star map that appears monthly in many newspapers to aid in your study of astronomy.

66. Have students follow articles on outer space exploration and choose specific topics for demonstration or oral presentation in class.

67. Have students create a dramatic bulletin board on the NASA space program, based on newspaper articles collected.

VI. SPACE FOR YOUR IDEAS

CHAPTER 13

Math

CONTENTS

Math

When students ask "Why do we have to learn so much math?" the teacher has only to point to the daily newspaper. An amazing amount of mathematical know-how is needed to get the most from the full range of information affecting our daily lives. Not only simple computation can be found in newspaper articles, but also fractions, percentages, ratios, comparison, and even the higher mathematical processes used to explain supply and demand economics. To convince students that the newspaper is full of math, start them off with a few quick games.

I. NUMBERS, TERMS, AND CONCEPTS

ACTIVITIES

1. Have students circle as many numbers as they can find on the front page in one minute. When the time is up, ask for a count.

2. Divide the class into teams for a scavenger hunt. The object is to find as many mathematics terms in the paper as possible in five minutes. For example: integer, fraction, decimal, rational and irrational number, mixed number, ratio, etc.

3. For another scavenger hunt, have them find as many math-related terms as possible in five minutes. For example: cost of living index, average, recession, inflation, percentage, down payment, etc. Compile a class list to post on the bulletin board and add to from time to time.

4. Have students search one page for all the terms that refer to time, such as annual, bicentennial, limited warranty, and yearly.

5. For a review, ask students to find all the numbers on page one that are odd, even, prime, divisible by 3, divisible by 7 or 9. Have them mark each differently so they can see which overlap and fit into more than one category.

6. Have a group develop a bulletin board of money-related articles. Discuss them weekly. Include cartoons that mention math.

7. Have students search the comics daily for mention of math concepts. Add a section of math humor to the bulletin board.

8. Have the class search the help wanted ads for jobs that require mathematical knowledge. Do any of them require a college degree in math or a related field?*

9. Use the numbers in a supermarket ad to practice "rounding off" to the nearest dollar, the nearest five dollars, etc.

10. Have students search the newspaper for palindromes, those numbers which read the same forward and backward. Ask them to select any number from the newspaper and decide if it is a palindrome. Circle as many as can be found. If a number is not a palindrome, simply reverse the digits and add them together. It may take several steps but the end result will be a palindrome. For example:

87	165	726	1353
+ 78	+ 561	+ 627	+ 3531
165	726	1353	4884

II. COMPUTATION
(roughly arranged in ascending order of difficulty)

ACTIVITIES

11. To review basic addition, have students locate a telephone number in the newspaper whose digits total 48.

12. Using any ads in the newspaper, including classified, have students plan to purchase at least three different items with no upper limit of items. The total amount of the purchases is to be exactly $500. Make this trickier by requiring that the $500 include whatever sales tax they must pay in your area.

13. Using the entertainment page, ask students to devise a schedule that would allow them to see as many movies in one day as possible. Be sure to allow travel time between theaters.

14. Have students compute the cost of taking their entire family out for an evening. Find an advertisement for a restaurant and determine the cost of dinner, including tip and tax. Select a movie, play, or concert to attend. What would be the total bill for the evening, including parking costs if any?

---

*Cross Reference: Chapter 15, "Career Education"

15. Use the travel section of the weekend paper to set up an itinerary and calculate costs for a trip. Encourage each student to plan a different trip and compare costs.

16. Have students select a full-page advertisement of sale items and determine the cost of purchasing everything on the page. Is there any way of determining how much you would save over the regular prices?

17. Using all the ads in the newspaper, ask students to discover two prices which differ by exactly five cents, ten cents, and two dollars.

18. Have students create a crossword puzzle using a full-page supermarket ad. The answers should be numbers. For example: 4 Across – How much change would be left from $1.00 after purchasing three cans of soup? 1 Down – The cost of three loaves of bread + one can of peas.

19. Using the travelers' exchange table on the financial pages, have students figure how much U.S. money they would need to exchange for different currencies, such as 100 English pounds, 1,000 French francs, 1,000 Argentine pesos, and 100 Japanese yen.

20. Find the coupon in the classified ads section that tells the cost per line or word. Choose a want ad and find out how much that ad cost for one day; for three days. How much can be saved by placing an ad for several days? How much would the whole page of ads cost at the three-day rate?

21. Have students select a classified ad that lists a salary and compute the rate of pay for an hour, day, week, month, and year.

22. Have students find an advertisement for medical or life insurance and compute the cost to them from age 18 to age 65.

23. Select a large group gathering students may have attended such as a concert. Using estimates, have them determine the total gate receipts for the event.

24. Tell students it takes approximately 14 pounds of newsprint to print 1,000 pages of newspaper. Based on this fact, determine the weight of newsprint used by your local daily newspaper each day. (*Hint:* circulation figures can be found in the masthead.)

25. Have students select from the classified ads an apartment they would like to live in. Compute the cost of the apartment for one year.

26. Looking at the weather report, ask students to determine which temperatures are multiples of 7, 8, or 9.

27. Using airline advertisements, have students determine the distance between two cities on the schedule and the cost per mile of making the trip.

28. Have students look at all the items under apartments for rent and determine the average number of bedrooms for apartments listed in today's paper.

29. Have students compute the average number of words on the front page of today's newspaper by measuring column inches of type and multiplying by the number of words in an average inch of type.

30. When the town or city budget is reported, ask students to create math problems from it. For example: How much will it cost each citizen to support the schools?[1]

31. Ask student to choose a full-page ad or flyer for a supermarket and determine the single-unit price for all items that are sold in multiples. Discuss why there cannot be a fraction of a penny.

32. The newspaper can offer some interesting averaging exercises. For example: wins and losses in sports; daily temperature or rainfall; age of men and women at death; birth rates; cost of renting a house.

33. Have students compute the cost of renting an apartment of their choice for ten years. Then compute the total payments for a house for ten years, using current mortgage costs. Debate which is the better system.[2]

34. Have students locate a business for sale which lists both the number of square feet in the building and the selling price. Compute the price per square foot for purchasing the business. Discuss how this would affect the cost of goods or services provided by the business.

35. Find a story about the salary paid to a sports figure. How much would that equal per game? How much per hour of play?

36. Teach students to determine unit prices from supermarket ads. For example: Is a 16-oz. box of cereal that sells for $.98 a better buy than a 24-oz. box that sells for $1.29?[3]

37. Create a chain calculation problem by using numbers from the newspaper. For example: multiply the volume number by the number of pages; divide by today's predicted high temperature; add the total of all points scored in last night's major league games; divide by today's winning lottery number. What is the answer?

38. Look at the automobile ads. Which costs the most? Which costs the least? What is the difference between the two? What is the average cost?

---

[1]**Cross Reference:** Chapter 11, "Social Studies": III. Government, H. Local Government
[2]**Cross Reference:** Chapter 14, "Consumer Education"
[3]*Ibid.*

39. Your class is given $250 to carpet a 12 x 18 section of the classroom. Cut out four carpeting ads and figure the cost per square yard for each carpet advertised and the total cost for each. Which carpet would you buy?

40. Find a newspaper ad for an airline which lists arrival and departure times. Determine the length of several trips in minutes, hours and minutes, and possibly seconds.

41. Ask students to clip all the coupons from the newspaper for a period of a week. Determine how much could have been saved if each coupon were used. Determine the amount of money paid for the newspapers for the week. How much net savings would be realized? Be sure to discuss how unlikely it would be that all the coupons would be used.

42. The masthead of the newspaper is the box which tells the ownership, gives circulation information, and lists subscription rates. Have students find the masthead and determine how much would be saved if the paper were purchased by subscription for one year instead of bought on a daily basis.

43. Ask students to look at the court report and determine the average age of defendants and the average fine paid. Conduct a class discussion to see if the age of the defendants had any relation to the amount of the fine. Does this project suggest that young people are arrested more frequently? Why might this be, or why not?[1]

44. Ask students to compile an estimate for putting paneling, new ceiling, and a carpet in your classroom, using newspaper advertising for the cost of each item.

III. WEIGHTS AND MEASURES

ACTIVITIES

45. Have students circle all references to measurement they can find in today's paper. Ask them to categorize each reference into measures of size, weight, distance, and volume.

46. Have students cut out any metric words they find in the newspaper and make a collage of them.

47. Have students compute the area of the front page and its perimeter. Do this in both English and metric measure.

---

[1]**Cross Reference:** Chapter 11, "Social Studies": IV. Sociology, A. Crime and Punishment

48. Have students measure the perimeter of the school property. Using ads for fencing from the newspaper, have them estimate the cost of fencing the entire school grounds. Do this in both English and metric measure.

49. Locate a rough blueprint drawing of a house in building ads or houses for sale ads. Ask students to determine the following:

    – The total area of the house

    – The perimeter of the house

    – The difference in area of the master bedroom from that of the others

    – The scale to which the drawing is made

50. Have students convert the temperature in today's weather report to Celsius.

51. Have students cut advertisements from the newspaper which give weights and measures. Glue these on paper so that equivalent amounts are on the same row separated by equal signs. For example:

    One gallon of milk = four quart jars of mayonnaise

52. Have students find ten items in the newspaper that are sold by the pound. Have them convert each of the prices to cost per ounce.

IV. FRACTIONS AND DECIMALS

ACTIVITIES

53. Have students search the newspaper for ten fractions and rewrite them as decimals. Then have students find ten decimals and rewrite them as fractions.

54. Have students try to find in the newspaper several ways to express the same fraction. For example: one half, ½, 50%, .50.

55. Ask students to use the panels of a cartoon strip to identify fractional parts. For example: one frame of a four-frame strip represents ¼. A word of caution: Not all cartoons have equal-sized panels.

56. Have students turn to the stock market report. Most of the numbers are listed there as mixed fractions. Have students rewrite each as an improper fraction.

V. PERCENTAGES AND GRAPHS

A. PERCENTAGES

ACTIVITIES

57. Ask students to select one advertisement for an item they would like to purchase. Ask them to calculate the amount of sales tax on the item.

58. If a real estate agent earns a 6 percent commission on the sale of a house, how much would an agent make selling five houses found in today's classified ads?

59. Ask each student to pretend he or she has opened a savings account for $500. Using bank advertisements, compute the amount of interest each would earn in three years. Are there other accounts that would offer a higher return on the money?

60. Encourage students to shop the newspaper for consumer loans. Ask them to determine how much interest they would have to pay based on bank and other advertising in the newspaper.[1]

61. Ask students to determine the percentage of space in the newspaper which is used for pictures; the percentage of space used for advertising.[2]

62. Have students find three ads for items which can be bought on time. For each of the items, figure the total finance charge that will be added to the purchase price. (Don't forget sales tax.) Conduct a class discussion on hidden costs in some purchases.[3]

63. Have students select a car they would like to purchase from the classified ads and determine the cost of monthly payments based on current lending rates.

64. Have students look at ads in the newspaper and note the list price and the sale price. Then have them determine the percentage of discount. If given a list price and a discount rate, they should determine the sale price; when given the sale price and the rate of discount, they should determine the original selling price.

65. Have students select an apartment they would like to live in and compute the cost of the rent for one year. Next have them locate a job in the classifieds for which they feel qualified. Compute the salary for one year. What percentage of the salary must be set aside for housing costs?

66. Select a help wanted ad which lists salary. Have students compute the weekly, monthly, and yearly totals. If 30 percent were deducted for taxes, insurance, etc., what would the take-home pay be?

---

[1]**Cross Reference:** Chapter 14, "Consumer Education"

[2]**Cross Reference:** Chapter 6, "Advertising"

[3]**Cross Reference:** Chapter 14, *op cit.*

67. Using newspaper advertising, ask students to determine how much an individual can place in an IRA (Individual Retirement Account) in one year. Ask them when the money will be taxable. If they placed $1,500 into an account annually, how much would be in the account at the end of the year? at the end of two years? (Remind them they would be earning interest on the first year's interest the second year.) Compute the total for twenty years.

68. Have students invest $10,000 in the stock market. They can buy and sell on a daily basis if they like. If you want to make the game more realistic, you may charge brokerage fees for buy and sell orders. At the end of an agreed time, determine who made the most money.

B. GRAPHS

ACTIVITIES

69. Have students keep an eye out for graphs appearing in the newspaper. (The *Wall Street Journal* has an abundance.) Ask students to interpret information from the graphs they find.

70. Go back to ACTIVITY 68 above and have students graph the amount of money they have on a daily basis.

71. Have students determine what percentage of the area of the newspaper is devoted to local news, national news, international news, sports, comics, editorial comment, classified advertising, display advertising, photographs, and illustrations. From this data, create a circle graph.[1]

72. Select a newspaper article which lists percentages of a whole such as reports of survey results. Ask students to read the article and from the information given, create a series of graphs which imparts the information correctly.

73. Ask students to underline every name found on the sports pages. Use red for the male names and green for the female names. Which are there more of? Determine the ratio of males to females. Do this for several days to see if the ratio changes. Design a graph to illustrate these ratios. Does this activity show a bias on the part of the newspaper?[2]

74. Collect a set of flyers from one supermarket for a period of time. Ask students to determine the changes in price for specific items over the time period. What was the percentage of change? Create a graph from the information obtained.

[1]**Cross Reference:** Chapter 1, "Getting Acquainted with the Newspaper": ACTIVITY 19
[2]**Cross Reference:** Chapter 11, "Social Studies": IV. Sociology

75. Ask students to create a line graph from weather statistics listed in the daily paper.

76. Have students compute the average daily temperature of several cities in the United States and make a bar graph using this information.

77. Have the class keep a record of sunrise and sunset for a period of time and make a graph showing the changes.

78. Turn to the TV listings. Ask students to find how many total hours of time are broadcast on one TV station. How much of that is devoted to news? Determine the percentage of time for several categories such as movies, comedies, drama, soap opera, game shows. Prepare a graph to show the results.*

VI. GEOMETRY

ACTIVITIES

79. Ask students to cut out as many examples of geometric shapes as they can find in today's newspaper. Make them into a bulletin board display.

80. Have students locate examples of parabolas and hyperbolas in the newspaper and outline the shapes with a magic marker.

81. Have students collect examples of platonic solids from the newspaper for a bulletin board display.

VII. COMPUTER TALK

ACTIVITIES

82. Have students create a program from the used car section of the classified ads that will do the following: determine average price, modal price, and median price.

83. Ask students to create a program to construct amortization tables for new homes.

84. Use the interest rates quoted in the newspaper bank advertisements to write a program which will calculate compound interest rates for a period of years.

*Cross Reference: Chapter 8, "The Newspaper Today": I. Have Radio and Television Made Newspapers Obsolete?

VIII. SPACE FOR YOUR IDEAS

CHAPTER 14

Consumer Education

CONTENTS

Consumer Education

Aimed as it is at the general populace and supported as it is by advertising, the newspaper is an ideal sourcebook for consumer education. Because many of the ACTIVITIES in Chapter 13, "Math," are inevitably consumer-oriented, referring to them individually here would become unwieldy. The teacher of consumer education should glance through the math ACTIVITIES as a supplement to those that follow here. Home economics, business education, industrial arts, and economics teachers will also find ACTIVITIES suited to their individual needs.

I. GENERAL CONSUMER ACTIVITIES

ACTIVITIES

1. Have students collect consumer advice columns and articles concerned with consumer issues. Divide the class into groups to consider topics according to the subtopics of this chapter. Have each group select several articles on a topic they consider especially pertinent and combine the class efforts for a bulletin board display. Add to the bulletin board on a regular basis, giving each group the responsibility of screening the week's collection of articles for the two or three most valuable.

2. Teachers of specific subject areas can modify the ACTIVITY 1 for their own subject.

3. Have students list consumer terms used in newspaper articles such as: market, save, research, buy, financial, expense, travel, claim. Keep a vocabulary of consumer terms found during news reading. Make a chart of these terms for the bulletin board and study their meanings.

4. Have students search newspapers for articles that discuss protection consumers receive from state and federal agencies. Have students list these agencies (for example, Federal Trade Commission, Food and Drug Administration, Department of Agriculture) and research their functions. Help students learn the extent of these agencies' powers and how rigorously they enforce their regulations.

5. Have students collect articles about non-governmental consumer protection organizations. Their job is then to list them, describe their range of activities, and evaluate their effectiveness.

6. Have students collect articles concerning organized consumer efforts to control the cost of living. Discuss the long- and short-term effectiveness of such actions.

II. PURCHASING

A. ADVERTISING: READING BETWEEN THE LINES

ACTIVITIES

7. Find an advertisement for an item that has been reviewed in *Consumer Reports* or a similar publication. Have students compare the report and the ad, then answer the question: Are all advertising claims justified?

8. Ask students to review the advertising in today's paper for hidden costs. For example: shipping charge, tax, installation, coupon required. Determine the complete price of each item.

9. Discuss the bait-and-switch trick with your students. What should they do if they discover this or other deceptive advertising practices?

10. Persuasion techniques are an important part of advertising. They are basically the same as propaganda techniques. Ask students to find examples of propaganda-type sales pitches in newspaper ads.[1]

11. Specialists in the Yale University psychology department have stated that the twelve most persuasive words in the English language are: **you, money, discover, results, save, new, easy, free, guarantee, health, love, proven.** Have students examine ads in the newspaper and circle those words wherever they appear. Which do they find used most often? Which do they think are most effective? Do they have any words they think should be added to the list?

12. Have students select the advertisement in today's newspaper they think is the **most** persuasive; the one they consider the **least** effective. From this activity, develop a list of characteristics for effective advertising. Follow up by having each student create an ad to sell a specific item.[2]

13. Logos or logotypes, the distinctive company signatures, symbols, or insignia, are an important part of some ads. This is especially true of national companies. Children can identify McDonald's golden arches before they can read a sign. Have students

---

[1]**Cross Reference:** Chapter 9, "English": II. Language, A. Semantics, ACTIVITY 53

[2]**Cross Reference:** Chapter 11, "Social Studies": V. Economics, ACTIVITY 124; Chapter 6, "Advertising: More Than Half the Paper," ACTIVITY 9

search newspapers for logos and write a brief explanation of why they think it is worth an advertiser's money to have a logo designed. (Logos can be as simple as a distinctive signature such as Ford's, the same since the Model T.)

14. Have students search in grocery and department store ads for examples of loss leaders. How does this method of advertising help the stores? What advantage, if any, can consumers take of this practice?

15. Invite the advertising manager of a large department store to class and have him or her explain the store's policies on warranties, returnable merchandise, loss leaders, and similar practices.

B. COMPARISON SHOPPING

ACTIVITIES

16. Have students select newspaper ads for products they would like and summarize the product information included in the ad. Evaluate the advertisement's adequacy as a basis for rational purchasing. Compile a list of all important questions, unanswered by the ad, they have about the product.

17. Have students use newspapers to find a product ad that includes a guarantee or a warranty. Evaluate the warranty by answering the following questions:

    – What is guaranteed?
    – Is the guarantee made by the seller, manufacturer, or service person?
    – How long is the guarantee effective?
    – What does the guarantee promise?
    – What must the consumer do to benefit from the guarantee?
    – What is the seller's policy concerning guarantees?

18. Have students consider that merchants seldom charge a round price like $1, $10, or $100. Why do they think they charge odd amounts like 97¢, $3.49, or $99?

1. Food

19. Have students collect articles on the economical purchase of food.

20. Have students plan a meal for a family, using supermarket ads to compute the cost.

21. Tell the students they have $50 ($60, $70) to feed a family of four for one week. Have each student plan purchases from newspaper ads. Discuss the plans with the entire class.*

*Cross Reference: Section III. Family Financing, C. Budgeting

22. Have students clip sale coupons from grocery store ads. Identify the coupons that are for products (not necessarily brand names) used frequently in their homes. Determine the total savings that would be realized through the use of all the coupons they have identified.

23. Have each student follow the price of a particular product, such as potatoes, over a period of weeks, then plot price fluctuations on a graph. See if students can determine reasons for price rises and declines.

24. Have students select a convenience food from a newspaper ad. Compare its price to the price of ingredients if it were made from scratch. After students have discussed this, ask them about the value of the time saved vs. the value of the experience of creating a tasty dish themselves. Under what circumstances would the cost of the convenience food be outweighed by the value of the time saved? Under what circumstances would the saving of money and the creative experience be more valuable?

2. Clothing and Furnishings

25. Using clothing advertisements from the newspaper, have students plan a seasonal wardrobe for themselves for $150. Divide into groups for comparison of purchases, and have each group choose the wardrobe with the most value for the money for presentation to the entire class.

26. Using home furnishings advertisements from the newspaper, have students choose a room in their houses to furnish or redecorate as economically, and at the same time, imaginatively as possible. Again divide into groups and follow the procedure in ACTIVITY 25 above.

27. Have students find and compare the cost of new appliances in store ads with the cost of used appliances in classifieds. Discuss the relative advantages of purchasing each.

28. After looking at clothing and furnishings ads, have students estimate the kind of purchase budgets they would need in these areas for a family of two, three, four, five.*

3. Shelter

29. Have students examine the housing ads in the classified section and do the following:

   — Define such terms as **lease, mortgage, prime interest rate**

   — Discuss abbreviations used

   — Discuss the hidden meaning in such descriptive phrases as:

      – extremely private location

*Cross Reference: Section III. Family Financing, C. Budgeting

- living room with new view
- oversize pine–finished bath

— Determine average cost for houses of similar size.

— Determine yearly cost of renting vs. yearly cost of buying.

30. Have students collect classified ads on either houses for sale or apartments for rent. Have them determine the average price of houses for sale or apartments for rent of one particular size or description.

31. Ask students to use information gathered in ACTIVITY 30 above for a discussion of advantages and disadvantages of buying vs. renting. Be sure they realize that basic mortgage cost or rental cost is only part of the financial commitment necessary.

32. Using the classified ads, have students figure the average cost per house for four different communities or four different parts of town. Have them make a bar graph comparing the average cost per house in the four areas.

4. Transportation

33. Have students compare used car advertisements to see if they can find a wide range of possible values.

34. Ask students to look at the **new** car ads in the newspaper and clip six different ads for cars they would like. Have them list the advantages and disadvantages of each car described and choose the best buy. They must give reasons why they made the choice.

III. FAMILY FINANCING

A. BORROWING

ACTIVITIES

35. Have students select a used car from the classified ads. Have them determine the payments for a specified length of time, using current bank financing rates. Determine the total finance charge.

36. Have students find several ads in the newspaper that offer credit terms. Determine the total amount paid for the product under the credit terms.

37. Have students find ads in the newspaper for finance companies and figure out the cost of interest per year. Compare with the interest rates for bank loans advertised by commercial and savings banks.

B. SAVING AND INVESTING

ACTIVITIES

38. Collect and file newspaper ads that encourage savings. Have students make their own collection. Ask them the following questions:

    - Which ads encourage savings?
    - How do the ads encourage savings?
    - What ads only appear to encourage savings?
    - What are the hidden costs?

39. Have students read and analyze in class columns from the financial pages dealing with investments, insurance, and Social Security.

40. Have students collect money market certificate ads. Does the interest vary from bank to bank? Ask students to list the ways in which different banks attempt to convince the customer that they offer the best deal. Compare these interest rates with other types of savings accounts.

41. Identify from the newspaper as many of the following terms as possible, and write down in a notebook the context in which each is used:

    - Bank savings accounts (passbook and certificates of deposit)
    - Corporate bonds
    - Common stocks
    - Government savings bonds
    - Free checking

C. BUDGETING

ACTIVITIES

42. Using information from the newspaper, ask students to construct a weekly budget for a family of four. Use wages listed in the classifieds for income figures.

43. Ask students to collect articles from the newspaper and to determine roughly how much it would cost for two people to live at a very basic level for one year. Calculate and add up the following:

    - Cost of food: determine a weekly average and multiply by 52
    - Cost of housing
    - Cost of clothing

– Cost of utilities
– Cost of transportation
– Cost of medical care
– Cost of entertainment

44. Have students determine the average salaries offered in the community according to classified ads for certain kinds of work, such as auto mechanic, secretary, clerk. Have them compare average salaries offered to women with those offered to men.

45. Have students prepare to debate this statement: It has been said that as many as fifty percent of the women who began to work in the 1970s are working out of necessity. After reading your newspaper and studying the cost of housing, food, and clothing (the three primary needs), determine if it can be argued that the head-of-household salary does not properly cover the expenses of such items. Or is it that luxuries have come to be regarded as necessities? Students may also prepare posters, using newspaper clippings, to defend either side of the argument.

IV. HOME MANAGEMENT

A. FOOD

ACTIVITIES

46. Have students collect articles on nutrition and dieting for group discussion and selection for a bulletin board display.

47. Have students make a special section of the bulletin board for new foods; for ethnic foods; for exotic recipes.

48. Have students collect articles on and discuss economical methods of food preparation. Have them test these methods at home or in the classroom.

49. Have students collect articles on different types of cooking methods, from wood stoves to microwave ovens. Divide into groups to plan presentations to the entire class on the advantages of each type.

50. Have students collect from the newspaper recipes that appeal to them for a personal cookbook. Encourage them to try the recipes whenever possible.

51. Have them choose recipes from the newspaper to practice enlarging or decreasing for larger or smaller families. Ask them to report which experiments were successful, which not.

52. Have each student choose a specialty and collect that kind of recipe for a personal cookbook.

B. CLOTHING

ACTIVITIES

53. Have students collect articles on fashion for a bulletin board display and for discussion. Ask how many of them see (or wear) the high style featured in many of these articles.

54. Have students plan a wardrobe from newspaper advertisements. The requirements are that it be useful, attractive, and within their budget (or the budget they would consider reasonable for someone their age in their community). Practicality is important. Ask them to be sure it fits their personal lifestyle. (See also ACTIVITY 25, page 242.)

55. Let students throw the puritan ethic to the winds and plan a wardrobe representing the style to which they would like to become accustomed from newspaper advertisements. (If you want to bring them back down to earth, have them add up the cost. If you want to let them dream on, skip it.)

C. FURNISHING AND DECORATING

ACTIVITIES

56. Have students find newspaper articles about home decorating and new fabrics. Discuss these frequently in class, calling to their attention the characteristics and advantages of new developments.

57. Using the information in the paper, both articles and ads, have students plan a redecoration scheme for a room of their home, or for an imaginary room they would like. (See also ACTIVITY 26, page 242.)

58. Have students locate in the classified ads everything they would need to furnish a small apartment for two. Give awards for the most imaginative, the most economical, and the most luxurious for the price.

59. Have students collect how-to articles on using found items to decorate. Discuss which ones would have lasting value and which would quickly lose their attraction. (This is, of course, a matter of taste, but creative use of unusual materials doesn't have to be tacky.)

D. HOME BUILDING AND MAINTENANCE

ACTIVITIES

60. Have students collect articles on all aspects of home planning and building. Working in groups, have them sort the articles into categories for a bulletin board, such as new construction, retrofitting, restoration of historic buildings, energy saving.

61. Have the class divide into groups to study different approaches to energy saving, using articles collected in ACTIVITY 60 above and looking further into their chosen topic. Plan a period for groups to present their areas of specialization to the class.

62. Have students collect pictures and floor plans of homes they would like from the Sunday supplement or daily papers and write or present orally a brief argument for their choice. They should consider both practical and aesthetic aspects.

63. Have students collect helpful hints from Heloise, home handyman and how-to articles, and the like for a classified bulletin board display, personal notebook, or poster.

64. Have students collect ads for new and used tools they would need to carry out chosen projects and compile a list of the best tools at the best prices.

65. Have students search the classified ads for used building materials and decide which ones would be good buys, which ones a waste of money, and why.

66. Have students look at the ads for building materials at supply houses and compare prices and quality of materials for a specific project.

67. Have students find in the classified ads contractors to do jobs they or their parents are unable to do around the home, select the ones they would employ, and tell why.

E. GROUNDS AND GARDENS

ACTIVITIES

68. Have students find articles on grounds maintenance (lawn mowing, snow removal, etc.), landscaping, flower and vegetable gardening, and indoor gardening. Discuss the values of learning as much as possible about these topics. Which ones are most important to different individuals? Have them defend their choices.

69. Have students choose a maintenance or gardening project, indoor or outdoor, that they would (or do already) enjoy and collect as much information about it as possible from the newspaper. Encourage them (or assign them, if feasible) to carry out a project they have discovered in the newspaper.

70. Have students find articles about growing their own food and discuss the pros and cons in class.*

F. CHILD CARE AND EDUCATION

ACTIVITIES

71. Have students find articles on baby and child care and related issues, such as day care centers. From the collection, have individual students or small groups choose areas of specialization for reports, collages, panel discussions, or posters.

72. Have students analyze toy advertisements in today's newspaper and rank the toys for suitability and safety.

73. Have students watch for articles on educational issues that affect their own lives, those of their younger brothers and sisters, or those of their future children. Choose several that arouse particular interest for class discussion or research.

---

*Cross Reference: Chapter 12, "Science": I. Biology, A. Plants, Animals, Ecology, Agriculture

G. RECREATION AND TRAVEL

ACTIVITIES

74. Have students find ads for equipment for their own favorite sports, hobbies, or family recreation. Compare features, quality, and prices. Have each student select the best buy in the area of his or her choice and tell why.

75. Have students plan a recreation or entertainment schedule for themselves, based on newspaper information on sports events, performing arts programs, or community recreation facilities such as Y programs.*

76. Have students plan a personal or family vacation—outdoor, city, abroad, adventure—based on ads and articles in the travel and recreation sections of the Sunday papers. Have them add up the cost, but don't let it spoil their fun.

*Cross Reference: Chapter 5, "Sports, Comics, and Other Special Features"; Chapter 10, "The Arts"

V. SPACE FOR YOUR IDEAS

Career Education

CONTENTS

Career Education

The newspaper is probably the most important single "source book" for career education. The Help Wanted section is the most obvious catalog of employment, but students should learn that many of the best jobs are not found there. Spend some time helping them to find clues to careers and specific jobs in articles about successful people, new businesses in your community, scientific discoveries, social service programs—government-sponsored, private, and volunteer—and dozens of other sources.

I. OCCUPATIONS

ACTIVITIES

1. How many occupations can students find listed on the front page? How many implied occupations? What types of jobs are mentioned most frequently in news stories?

2. Have students survey the comics page. How many occupations are listed there? Are they portrayed realistically? How many are stereotypes?*

3. Ask each student to select a photograph from the newspaper and list all the jobs which can be associated with the picture.

4. Have students find columns and special features directly about career opportunities, as well as others from which they can draw inferences about career possibilities.

5. Have students create special jobs that would help solve unusual problems they find in news stories. This activity could be humorous or serious, or a combination of both. Sometimes the best brainstorming can come from facetious suggestions that spark really good ideas.

6. Ask each student to choose one of the subjects he or she is currently taking and find as many occupations as possible mentioned in the newspaper which use skills learned in that subject.

7. Have students arrange the jobs in today's classified ads from highest to lowest in terms of public contact. Ask them to determine for themselves how much public contact

*Cross Reference: Chapter 9, "English": II. Language, A. Semantics, ACTIVITY 49

they would like for their own employment. Use this same format for several other job criteria.

8. Discuss journalism as a career. It has been described as "usually ego-satisfying, a public service, and often exciting." It is often considered a good training ground for other forms of creative writing. What are some other aspects of a journalism career as perceived by students? Do they find any journalism jobs listed in the Help Wanted columns? Why or why not?

9. Have students find listings of part-time jobs. Ask them to suggest advantages and disadvantages of part-time employment.

10. Have students create a classroom career file. Place each Help Wanted ad on a 3 x 5 card. Categorize these by types of jobs. After the file has been developed for some time, ask students to make some inferences. Which jobs are most plentiful? Which job is hardest to get? Are job opportunities increasing or decreasing? etc.

11. Have students find five different kinds of jobs advertised in the Help Wanted ads. Try to find one from each of these categories: clerical, technical, professional, domestic, sales. Have them write a short paragraph about what they think a typical day would be like in each job.

II. QUALIFICATIONS

ACTIVITIES

12. Have students check the Help Wanted columns and make a list of the types of employment available in your community. Have them work in groups to record how many require experience, how many require a high school diploma, how many require specific training or previous experience, how many require a college degree, how many state age requirements and salaries. Have groups put their findings together on a chart for the bulletin board.

13. Ask students to clip ads from the classifieds for jobs they would like to have. Ask them to determine the following information for each job: salary, hours, advancement possibilities, education required. If any of this information was missing from the ad, have students try to guess why.

III. EQUAL OPPORTUNITY

ACTIVITIES

14. Students need encouragement to be assertive in following their career choices. Discuss stereotyping, the Equal Rights Amendment, Title IX, and other civil rights legislation as it relates to the job market.

15. Have students find articles about people, especially women, who have broken the barriers of stereotyping to pursue unusual careers.

16. Have students collect clippings of articles about job discrimination. After a period of collecting, have students work in groups on different areas or specific cases to prepare reports to present to the class for general discussion. For example, it took eleven years to resolve a class action suit by women journalists against the Associated Press on charges of sexual and racial discrimination.

17. Have students select a job ad which includes the phrase "equal opportunity employer" and write an essay on what this means.

IV. FINDING JOBS

ACTIVITIES

18. Have students collect Help Wanted ads from newspapers in several different cities in your state or region. Which city seems to have the most jobs of the type they would like? What factors would they consider before moving to that city? Do the same with Help Wanted ads from papers across the country.

19. Have students find a Help Wanted ad which was placed by an employment agency. Have them discover how a private employment agency works.

20. Have students write an ad for the Positions Wanted section of classifieds. Discuss what makes a good ad.

V. APPLYING FOR JOBS

ACTIVITIES

21. Have students find a job in the Help Wanted section that they would like to have and write a letter of application describing their qualifications.

22. As practice for writing letters of application, have students pretend to be a doctor, nurse, firefighter, executive secretary, teacher, etc., and write a paragraph about themselves including the Five Ws:

    - Who: your name
    - What: your occupation
    - Where: urban, rural, etc.
    - Why: reasons you chose that job
    - When: when you could start
    - How: how much education you have

23. Have students select jobs in the classifieds they would like to have and work in pairs practicing interviews with prospective employers. The ad should include skills and other requirements for the job. Afterward, have each interviewer tell the applicant whether he or she would have been hired and why.

24. Have students choose a career they might like to train for and prepare to go job hunting in that field. Have them look at a number of ads and decide which qualifications are most in demand. Work with them in writing résumés of their imagined training and experience for prospective employers.

VI. SPACE FOR YOUR IDEAS

APPENDIX

SOURCES OF INFORMATION

Newspaper in Education

American Newspaper Publishers Association Foundation
The Newspaper Center
Box 17407, Dulles International Airport
Washington, DC 20041   (703) 620-9500

Bibliography (excellent source of dozens of helpful publications)

Directory of Participating Newspapers (by states)

Brochures listing new publications

First Amendment Congress

ANPA Foundation
Box 17407, Dulles International Airport
Washington, DC 20041

Publishes newsletter; Judith Hines, Secretary

Reporters Committee for Freedom of the Press

800 18th Street NW
Washington, DC 20006

Publishes quarterly magazine: *The News Media and the Law* (full coverage of every incident involving confrontation between the press and the law)

Sigma Delta Chi, Professional Journalistic Society

25 East Wacker Drive
Chicago, IL 60601

Material on careers in journalism

Maine State Newspaper in Education Program

Department of Educational and Cultural Services
State House Station 23
Augusta, ME 04333   (207) 289-2541

Pamphlets:

"The Substitute's Friend: A Guide to Uses of the Daily Newspaper by Classroom Substitutes"

"Parents and Papers: Partners in Education"

Many other materials

Canadian Daily Newspaper Publishers Association

321 Bloor Street East
Toronto, Ontario M4W 1E7

TELEVISION:

All news programs and special documentaries

    60 Minutes – CBS

    Front Line – PBS

Specials:

    The Constitution, A Delicate Balance – PBS (1983 series, probably will be repeated)

    The Ascent of Man – PBS (series already repeated several times)

RADIO:

    Options – PBS (includes many documentaries, including National Press Club meetings)

FILMS:

    Under Fire (1983) The role of journalists in the Nicaraguan revolution

    Absence of Malice (1982) A dramatic probe of journalism's ethics

    All the President's Men (1974) The Watergate episode

    Medium Cool (1969) How the media handled the Chicago Democratic Convention riots of 1968

    Citizen Kane (1941) Fiction based on the life of William Randolph Hearst

    The Front Page (1931) The heyday of Chicago newspaper life

AUDIOVISUAL MATERIALS:

Educational Films and Filmstrips

Sources:

Current Affairs
P.O. Box 426
Ridgefield, CT 06877

Getting Started in Journalism by Gillespie and Engebretson (see BIBLIOGRAPHY, page 265) contains an excellent list of audiovisual materials and their sources.

Indiana University Audio Visual Center
Bloomington, Indiana 47405

AV MATERIALS LISTED BY CHAPTER

(IU = order from Indiana University; CA = order from Current Affairs; see page 260.)

Chapter 1: THE NEWSPAPER ITSELF

How to Read Newspapers: Briefly views parts of newspaper; how to read critically; jobs of various staff members; fact vs. opinion. 13 min. sd. col. (1970) IU

News: Communications: Features well–known journalists discussing language vs. visual material; importance of precision, accuracy; slanting. 15 min. sd. col. (1977) IU

Newspaper Story: Follows one edition of the *Los Angeles Times* through process of news gathering, writing, editing, printing, delivery. 27 min. sd. col. (1970) IU

Your Daily Newspaper: A Modern Marvel of Printing Technology: Follows newsgathering, editorial, and production processes, using latest technology. Filmstrip. sd. col. Purchase. CA

Wood Blocks and Metal Type: Follows the history of printing to modern letterpress. 29 min. sd. B & W. IU

Chapter 2: WHAT IS NEWS?

Critical Thinking: Making Sure of Facts: Demonstrates need to check sources of information; presents three different accounts of same event; difference between fact and statement of fact. 11 min. sd. col. (1971) IU

News: A Closer Look: Features well-known journalists discussing what is honest reporting, how objective news is, what limits TV news. 15 min. sd. col. (1977) IU

News: Communications: See Chapter 1 above.

The News: A Free Press: Features famous journalists examining factors affecting freedom and objectivity, bias, how a free press affects other freedoms, reporters' personal professional guidelines. 15 min. sd. col. (1977) IU

The News: What Is It? Features well–known journalists examining roles of writers, editors, columnists, procedures, news values, public's wants; compares print/electronic media. 15 min. sd. col. (1973) IU

The Newspaper: Today's Model for Clear and Concise Writing: Illustrated activities demonstrating writing techniques. Filmstrip. sd. col. Purchase. CA

The Newspaper and Your Quest for Truth: Demonstrates differences between straight news and interpretive reporting, reader's responsibility in determining truth, propaganda techniques, credibility gap. Filmstrip. sd. col. Purchase. CA

What Is a Good Observer? Considers differences between good and bad observation, techniques for thorough observing. 30 min. sd. B & W. (1961) IU

Chapter 3: FEATURES: THE OTHER KIND OF NEWS

The Newspaper: Today's Model for Clear and Concise Writing: See Chapter 2 above.

What Is a Good Observer? See Chapter 2, page 261.

Chapter 4: THE EDITORIAL PAGES: MATTER OF OPINION

News: What Is It? See Chapter 2, page 261.

The Newspaper and Your Quest for Truth: See Chapter 2, page 261.

Shaping the News for the Consumer: How news media decide what news will be reported and how. 17 min. sd. col. (1975) IU

The Tiger's Tail: Thomas Nast vs. Boss Tweed: Exciting story of how cartoonist Thomas Nast helped break the corrupt Tweed ring in New York in the 1870s. 20 min. sd. B & W. (1953) IU

Chapter 5: SPORTS, COMICS, AND OTHER SPECIAL FEATURES

The Tiger's Tail (for cartoons): See Chapter 4 above.

TV News: Measure of the Medium: Discusses sources, ways events can be presented, selectivity of camera angle, graphics (for photojournalism), distortion by omission, race against time, etc. 14 min. sd. col. (1971) IU

Chapter 6: ADVERTISING: MORE THAN HALF THE PAPER

The Business of Newspapers: Examines past, present, and future of newspaper responsibility and problems, how coverage is influenced by economics, loss of independence to economic forces. 43 min. sd. col. (1978) IU

News: The Business: Financial needs of newspapers; importance of advertising; influence of advertisers on editorial opinion; manipulation of consumer. 15 min. sd. col. (1977) IU

Chapter 7: NEWS AND HISTORY

Eyewitness: Wild West journalism, including Horace Greeley, Sam Clemens, Bret Harte, and Teddy Roosevelt. 30 min. sd. B & W. (1964) IU

Freedom of the Press: A Priceless Heritage: History of freedom of the press, censorship, modern editorial responsibility. Filmstrip. col. sd. Purchase. CA

Mightier Than the Sword: Zenger and Freedom of the Press: Dramatizes the 1734 court case that first used truth as a defense against libel. 23 min. sd. B & W. IU

This Is Edward R. Murrow: Career of famous newsman: his confrontation with Senator Joseph McCarthy, interviews with presidents, etc. 44 min. 2 reels. sd. B & W. (1976) IU

This Is Marshall McLuhan: The Medium Is the Message: Presents McLuhan's thoughts on power of media to change perception. 53 min. B & W. sd. (1968) IU

The Tiger's Tail: See Chapter 4 above.

Wood Blocks and Metal Type: See Chapter 1, page 261.

Chapter 8: THE NEWSPAPER TODAY

The Bill of Rights in Action: Freedom of the Press: Considers constitutional issues regarding news leaks and reporters' privilege to refuse to name sources. 21 min. sd. col. IU

The Business of Newspapers: See Chapter 6 above.

Censorship: A Question of Judgment: Dramatizes disagreement between a high school reporter and a principal; leaves solution to audience. 5 min. sd. col. (1964) IU

Freedom of the Press: A Priceless Heritage: See Chapter 7, page 262.

Free Press/Fair Trial: Conflict between right to know and fair trial; Agnew's claim that press convicted him, and other cases. 30 min. sd. B & W. (1973) IU

Getting the News: Documents various roles of radio, TV, and newspaper bringing the same event to the public. 15 min. sd. col. (1967) IU

Journalism: Mirror, Mirror on the World: Analyzes and compares coverage of peace demonstration by Public Broadcasting, David Brinkley (NBC), *Washington Post, New York Times,* UPI. Shows final story of each. 52 min. 2 reels. sd. col. IU

Mass Media: Power and Responsibility: Rapid evolution of mass media and the questions it evokes on freedom of press, right to know, censorship. Filmstrip. sd. col. Purchase. CA

News: The Business: See Chapter 6, page 262.

News: A Closer Look: See Chapter 2, page 261.

The News: A Free Press: See Chapter 2.

News: What Is It? See Chapter 2.

The Newspaper and Your Quest for Truth: See Chapter 2.

The Paper Sword: Story of 1850 murder of James King, a newspaper editor who exposed corruption in government; how his murder incited reform.

Privacy Under Attack: Personal privacy vs. freedom of the press and the public's right to know. Filmstrip. sd. col. Purchase. CA

Shaping the News: See Chapter 4, page 262.

This Is Edward R. Murrow: See Chapter 7, page 262.

TV News: Measure of the Medium: See Chapter 5, page 262.

The Whole World Is Watching: David Brinkley and Walter Cronkite discuss with critics TV bias and how they strive for fairness. 55 min. sd. B & W. (1969) IU

Chapter 9: ENGLISH

Critical Thinking: See Chapter 2, page 261.

The Newspaper: Today's Model for Clear and Concise Writing: See Chapter 2.

The Newspaper and Your Quest for Truth: See Chapter 2.

This Is Marshall McLuhan: See Chapter 7, page 262.

Chapter 10: THE ARTS

Chapter 11: SOCIAL STUDIES

BIBLIOGRAPHY

Ayer Directory of Publications, 1983. Fort Washington, PA: IMS Press, 1983.

Bagdikian, Ben. *The Media Monopoly.* Boston: Beacon Press, 1983.

Bettleheim, Bruno. *The Uses of Enchantment.* New York: Alfred A. Knopf, 1976.

Bibliography: Newspaper in Education Publications, 4th Ed. Washington, DC: American Newspaper Publishers Association Foundation, 1982.

Bronowski, Jacob. *The Ascent of Man.* Boston: Little, Brown and Company, 1973.

Emery, Edwin. *The Press and America.* Englewood Cliffs, NJ: Prentice-Hall, Inc., 1972.

Gillespie, Jack, and Herschel O. Engebretson. *Getting Started...in Journalism.* Glassboro, NJ: Educational Impact, Inc., 1973.

Hayakawa, S.I. *Language in Thought and Action.* New York: Harcourt, Brace and World, Inc., 1964.

McLuhan, Marshall. *Understanding Media: The Extensions of Man.* New York: McGraw-Hill Book Company, 1964.

Miller, Bobby Ray, ed. *The UPI Handbook.* New York: United Press International, 1977.

The Newspaper as an Effective Teaching Tool. Washington, DC: American Newspaper Publishers Association Foundation, 1977.

Pickett, Calder M. *Voices of the Past.* New York: John Wiley and Sons, Inc., 1984.

Pocket Pal: A Graphic Arts Production Handbook, 11th ed. New York: International Paper Company, 1976.

Rifkin, Ira, "The News Is Wired." *Focus: Media.* San Franciso: Chandler Publishing Co., 1972.

Ritter, Jess, and Grover Lewis, eds. *Focus: Media.* San Francisco: Chandler Publishing Co., 1972.

Seitz, Don C. *Joseph Pulitzer: His Life and Letters.* New York: Simon and Schuster, 1924.

Thomsen, William F. *Media and Communication.* New York: Harcourt Brace Jovanovich, Inc., 1972.

READING LIST
A Few Biographies and Adventures of Journalists

Anderson, Dave, ed. *The Red Smith Reader.* New York: Random House, 1982.

Anderson, Jack, with James Boyd *Fiasco.* New York. Times Books, 1983.

Baker, Russell. *The Rescue of Miss Haskell and Other Pipe Dreams.* New York: Congdon and Weed, 1983.

Deakin, James. *Straight Stuff: The Reporters, the White House and the Truth.* New York: William Morrow and Company, Inc., 1984.

Dugger, Ronnie. *On Reagan: The Man and His Presidency.* New York: McGraw–Hill Book Company, 1983.

George, F.W. *The Pursuit of Virtue and Other Tory Notions.* New York: Simon and Schuster, Inc., 1983.

Geyer, Georgie Anne. *Buying the Night Flight: The Autobiography of a Woman Correspondent.* New York: Delacorte, 1983.

Goodman, Ellen. *At Large.* New York: Fawcett Crest, 1981.

Hentoff, Nat. *The First Freedom: The Tumultuous History of Free Speech in America.* New York: Delacorte, 1980.

_____ . *The Day They Came to Arrest the Book.* New York, Delacorte, 1982.

May, Antoinette. *Witness to War: A Biography of Marguerite Higgins.* New York: Beaufort Books, Inc., 1983.

McNeil, Robert. *The Right Place at the Right Time.* Boston: Little, Brown and Company, 1982.

Swanberg, W.A. *Citizen Hearst.* New York: Scribners, 1961.

_____ . *Pulitzer.* New York: Scribners, 1967.

Trillin, Calvin. *Killings.* New York: Ticknor and Fields, 1984.

_____ . *Uncivil Liberties.* Garden City, NY: Anchor Books, 1983.

White, William Allen. *The Autobiography of William Allen White.* New York: Macmillan, 1946.

Wolfe, Tom. *The Purple Decades, A Reader.* New York: Berkley Books, 1982.

_____ . *The Right Stuff.* New York: Bantam, 1980.

_____ , and E.W. Johnson. *The New Journalism.* New York: Harper and Row, 1973.

Woodward, Bob, and Carl Bernstein. *All the President's Men.* New York: Simon and Schuster, 1974.